Towards Enchantment

Towards Enchantment

Exploring Consciousness and the
Afterlife Through Physics, Philosophy,
and Parapsychology

Rachel Meisler Zirlin

For my parents, Sylvia and Harold,
who allowed me the intellectual freedom to explore.

And for my daughters and granddaughter,
who help make this slice of space-time meaningful.

Contents

Preface

I am sitting cross-legged, floating above my bed near the ceiling. I am four or five years old. This has happened several times, maybe three, over the year. When I tell my parents about it, they assure me it was only a dream. And perhaps it was, but it felt so real. Whether or not this was the beginning of my spiritual journey, I do not remember. I do know that my search for metaphysical truth, in one form or another, has been a central theme for most of my life.

Can a person break free from their metaphysical paradigm or worldview and approach objective truth without it being filtered through the lens of family, upbringing, education, society, and life experiences? Probably not, or not entirely. These forces shape patterns of thought and perception, molding the way we interpret reality, a process known as conditioning. As Dean Radin states, "We do not perceive the world as it is, but [...] we construct mental models of a world that reflect our expectations, biases, and desires, a world that is comfortable for our egos, that does not threaten our beliefs, and that is consistent, stable, and coherent" (Radin 1997, p. 229). We each create a personal paradigm, a philosophical or theoretical framework through which we perceive the world. This is true of philosophers, scientists, and just ordinary folks.

I have known many people who could no more entertain the idea of a world without God or an afterlife than they could deny the evidence of their own senses. Such an idea would not fit within their worldview and would be incomprehensible to them. I have also known people on the opposite end of the spectrum for whom the idea of a spiritual reality or an afterlife is completely absurd. Ask around. Many of your friends, family, and acquaintances likely fall into one of these camps or the other.

My own worldview has taken many twists and turns, often changing dramatically—sometimes to the dismay of my family. So in my case, I did alter my metaphysical worldview multiple times. It is easier when you're young, as are most things. Whether I approached objective truth is an entirely different question. This book is an account of those twists and turns and an attempt to "think on paper" (or laptop), and perhaps come to some conclusions. Or not.

To my friends and family reading this: Some of you may find the ideas in this book absurd. Others may see my conclusions as obvious. Some of you may find the book thought-provoking, and others may be bored. Some may even find certain ideas here offensive. And for some, my ideas may resonate and lead you in new philosophical directions. This book is simply the story of my lifelong metaphysical quest and my conclusions as they stand now. As Carl Sagan said, "Of course, I could be wrong."

One

Looking Back

Early Years. I remember being fascinated when my parents read to me from a children's book of Jewish Bible stories. My parents were not believers—far from it. They read the stories as fiction or fairy tales, and from a cultural perspective. Both my parents were atheists, as were three of my four grandparents. I don't think I realized that Jews believed in God until I was nine or ten.

Nevertheless, I was fascinated by the religion of others and the magic of Christmas pervasive in the wider culture. For some reason, I was especially taken with *A Charlie Brown Christmas,* which played annually on broadcast

TV. At some point in my preteen years, I created a small religious altar with figurines in a shoebox, which I kept hidden in a closet. I have never shared the story of my shoebox altar until now. It likely would have met with tacit disapproval, and even now, the memory brings a sense of embarrassment.

Also, during my childhood, the concept of death was not discussed. Neither did anyone speak of an afterlife. I assume they believed that death is the end of the person. When it's over, it's over. One day when I was seven years old, I walked into the kitchen and found my father crying. I think it was the first time I had ever seen him cry. He and my mother told me that my uncle Irving, my father's older brother, had passed away. I thought that meant he passed out. It was almost a year till I understood that he had died. I do remember great feelings of sympathy at the demise of any dead fly I happened upon and wondering where they went after death. (Curiously, I liked flies. Ugly, crawly bugs, not so much.)

Despite my parents' obvious secular rationalism, my upbringing was not completely devoid of spiritual leanings. My father was a lover of music and art. He collected antiques of Hindu, Buddhist, and medieval Christian origin. In later years, he listened to sitar music and established a practice of meditation.

Were our metaphysical inclinations the natural response of our brains? Quite a few studies suggest that the brain may be hardwired for spirituality. Dr. Michael Persinger (1945–2018), a neuroscientist who ran the Consciousness Research Lab at Laurentian University in Sudbury, Ontario, focused much of his work on the neural correlates of psychic and spiritual perceptions, particularly in relation to temporal lobe seizure activity. He contended that electromagnetic fields present in the environment, both natural and manufactured by human activity, create changes in the brain that lead to hallucinations and mystical experiences. According to Persinger, it is these fields that may cause "haunting" phenomena at certain electromagnetically active locations. And, indeed, he did find a high level of electromagnetic field (EMF) activity in several locations of hauntings involving sounds and apparitions (Roach 2006, chap. 9).

At the lab, Persinger created a soundproofed room and an electromagnetically wired helmet that would generate and control EMFs. He demonstrated statistically significant results, which suggested that EMFs created the perception of paranormal activity in subjects wearing the helmet. (His findings have not been replicated.) From the title of his book *Neuropsychological Bases of God Beliefs* (1987), one would think he concluded that psychic and spiritual perceptions are "all in the brain." However, correlation does not imply causation. (For example, the correlation between windmill velocity and wind velocity doesn't mean that windmills cause wind.) It is just as plausible that certain environmental and brain states allow spiritual perceptions that would not be ordinarily accessible. In fact, Persinger himself allowed for the idea that psychic phenomena are possible (Roach 2006, pp. 120–121).

Another reason our brains may be "hardwired" for spirituality would be evolution. Spirituality and organized religion probably have an evolutionary advantage.

Religion provides social structure and cohesion, which in turn provides a survival advantage. In addition, according to paleoanthropologist Bridget Alex, "Many mental ingredients are necessary for religion as-we-know-it. But scholars emphasize three tendencies in particular, which are pronounced in humans, but minimally expressed in other species: We seek patterns, infer intentions and learn by imitation" (Alex 2018). These tendencies would provide a significant survival benefit. Particularly the inferring of intentions, according to Alex, would also allow humans to attribute thought to inanimate objects, animals, and forces of nature.

Many articles citing the evolutionary and neurological underpinnings of spirituality seem to imply that because spirituality can be found in the brain, the brain is the only source of spirituality—that there can be no objective truth to spiritual notions. Conversely, articles written by authors of a more spiritual bent, such as Christian De Quincy (2003), imply that the brain has evolved (or been created) to detect an actual spiritual reality or truth, just as the visual cortex evolved to see actual objects in the environment. So the question arises: Is spirituality merely an experience generated by the brain? Or has the brain evolved to detect an objective spiritual reality? In other words, just because we are hardwired to believe in a greater reality, that doesn't mean it's real, and it doesn't mean it isn't.

In my preteens, I was not contemplating intellectual arguments for and against the existence of a spiritual reality or an afterlife. It was understood in my family that intelligent people did not believe in such things. I do recall a particular experience, however, that may have portended my lifelong questioning of the nature of self and reality. Perhaps most people have similar experiences and never describe them to anyone. I didn't—until right now. I was probably about eleven or twelve years old, and I recall looking at myself in the mirror and having an almost ineffable experience of myself as consciousness. Who/what is the person who is me and no one else? In *36 Arguments for the Existence of God,* a novel by philosopher (and avowed atheist) Rebecca Goldstein, the protagonist, Cass, describes a "metaphysical seizure." He first experiences this as a boy, and it continues into adulthood:

> How can it be that of all things, one is *this* thing, so that one can say, astonishingly—in the right frame of mind, it *is* astonishing, with the metaphysical chill blowing in from afar—"here I am?" (Goldstein 2010)

Venturing Out. My "hardwired" spirituality came out in full force during ninth grade. I was fourteen, and it was the early '70s. The Jesus movement was at its height. The *Time* magazine cover for June 21, 1971, was entitled "The Jesus Revolution," and the "Jews for Jesus" movement was just beginning. Political correctness was not yet a thing, nor was diversity or sensitivity training. Parents did not "helicopter," nor did they "manage" their children's teachers. They were not as litigious as they are today. This perfect storm is what propelled me into the Jesus movement.

I was born in the middle of the baby boom, and there were so many students in my school district that the junior high and high schools were divided into three separate buildings. There were no middle schools at that time. The seventh and eighth grades were in one building, ninth and tenth in a second, and eleventh and twelfth in a third. In ninth grade at Charles Boehm School (now a middle school), I encountered three biology teachers in the same department who were evangelical Christians: Steve Myers, Thomas Clegg, and the third whose name I've forgotten. The arguments of a fourteen-year-old were no match for their intellectual rhetoric.

During biology class, which I loved (in addition to history and English), Mr. Myers discussed the theory of evolution as "only a theory." Of course, I realize now that this argument is sophomoric, but hey, I wasn't even a high school sophomore. I was confused, intrigued, and shocked that an intelligent person, a man of science, believed in a god.

Mr. Thomas Clegg, in particular, was an extremely charismatic man with dancing eyes and an infectious laugh. He was an evangelical Quaker whose ideas were heavily influenced by the Christian apologists C.S. Lewis and, especially, Francis Schaeffer, who at the time ran a fellowship retreat/community in Switzerland. Mr. Clegg had a keen intellect—at least to my teenage mind—and his philosophical arguments for the existence of God were very persuasive. It was he who sparked my interest in philosophy.

My mind was filled with a heady mixture of thoughts that included words such as presupposition, paradigm, mechanistic, reductionist, and logical consistency. I could go on. I think the argument that spoke to me the most was the moral argument for God and the thought that believing in morality was somehow inconsistent with atheism. Existentialist literature, or my interpretation of it at the time, convinced me that life would be without meaning and morality if there were no God. I now wholeheartedly reject this argument.

The three biology teachers ran a Bible study for high school students out of a local Quaker church, and I was invited. Within a month, much to the dismay of my parents, I was converted. I can't say why I took an immediate leap from accepting the possibility that there could be a god, across the chasm into Christianity. Clearly, my intellectualism was not what I thought.

My parents told me they assumed I was just rebelling and looking to be part of a group for a sense of belonging. There may have been some of that. Certainly, the idea of being a quasi-hippie "Jesus Freak" with the requisite ripped-up bell-bottom jeans was appealing. Pictures of Francis Schaeffer's community, L'Abri in Switzerland, complete with photos of long-haired young people sitting about looking "intellectual," were also enticing. I do think that my primary motivation was my spiritual and intellectual seeking. My parents, although likely appalled, held a laissez-faire approach to parenting towards both me and my brother Andy. They even sometimes drove me to the Bible study meetings.

I continued in my Christianity throughout high school and halfway through college. I attended one semester at a state university, and, miserable and homesick, I returned home. My parents probably didn't know what to do with me, and so I was able to talk them into allowing me to attend a Christian college—Gordon College in Massachusetts, where I majored in English and minored in philosophy. I flourished there, both socially and intellectually, and it was there that I became disillusioned with Christianity and religion in general. All my youthful arguments for the existence of God crumbled.

The first thing to go was the concept that those who did not believe were destined for eternal damnation. This would include children, aboriginal people in primitive cultures, and all who were raised in other faiths and were unable to change their worldview. That concept became completely untenable, objectionable, and inconsistent with the concept of a just and loving God.

Then there was the idea of God sacrificing his son for our sins. What does human sacrifice have to do with saving everyone from sin? And if human suffering atoned for sins, why couldn't our own ubiquitous suffering suffice (famine, disease, war, pain, loss, etc.)? Did God need to send part of himself to earth as his son to be sacrificed to himself so he could persuade himself to forgive us? Why does he require sacrifice to forgive us for behaving the way he created us? Couldn't he just decide to forgive? The concept of sacrifice to appease the gods predates Christianity and can be seen throughout history and prehistory, especially in the Americas and parts of the Middle East. There is some evidence from archaeology that the practice of sacrifice contributed to the development of hierarchical social structures. The practice came to be viewed as barbaric in most of the world, but it continues on with the idea of God's sacrifice of his son.

I began to question the idea of God as the basis for morality. Morality as seen in Christianity, and in the world's religions in general, is just as variable and relativistic as the morality of agnosticism or atheism. The Bible itself (particularly the Old Testament) is filled with laws that are either silly (it is not allowed to wear clothing made of both linen and wool) or reprehensible, including allowing for slavery and dictating the cutting off of transgressors' hands. Did the God of the Old Testament change his mind for the New Testament? Is there a reason we should assume God's proclamations are the moral ones, rather than relying on our own human judgments of right and wrong, which often seem much more moral than those of various scriptures? The behavior of religious people throughout history and throughout the world is certainly no better than the behavior of non-believers. Even the religious person must interpret the scriptures and decide for themself which laws to follow and how.

So where does morality come from? Well, from a humanist point of view, it comes from within humanity itself—our society, our evolution, and our nature. Humanists make "their ethical decisions based on a concern for the welfare of human beings and other sentient animals [shout out to my dog, Darwin] and to make a positive contribution towards building a better society" ("What Is Humanism? » Understanding Humanism," n.d.). The Golden Rule (which can be found in the Bible) says to do unto others as you would have them do unto you, which is a good place to start. The Wiccan Rede, "If it harm none, do what you will," is similar, as is the concept of karma. Put another way, "Don't be an a**h***; be a *mensch*" (Yiddish for decent human being). The point is that each theory of morality is based on a presupposed concept, whether it be God, humanity, or something else.

I also questioned the *cosmological argument*, which says that there must be a first cause for everything that exists. This raises the question: What or who caused God? The philosopher Gottfried Wilhelm Leibniz (1646–1716) asked, "Why is there something rather than nothing?" What would nothing even look like? It is unimaginable, and like a Zen koan, the question is unanswerable.

And finally, there is the question of where one derives meaning in life. For the humanist, meaning is "informed by evidence, inspired by empathy, and infused with hope and wonder for the world around us" ("What Is Humanism? » Understanding Humanism," n.d.). This is not to say that I embraced humanism during this part of my life. I just did not feel the necessity for a god to give my life a sense of meaning. I was also skeptical of the idea that logic or reason could find answers to life's ultimate questions. So for now, like Voltaire's Candide, I would cultivate my own garden.

I found myself in my last year and a half at Gordon College in the uncomfortable position of being an agnostic at a Christian school. However, I soldiered on and completed my degree at Gordon, keeping my thoughts mostly to myself and enjoying my social life and studies in general. My focus turned to my friendships, my future, and my continuing pursuit of the male of the species.

After graduation, I spent a year working as a secretary at a publishing company and taking acting classes for fun. I then enrolled in a master's degree program in speech pathology at Columbia University. I did not pursue further academic studies in literature or philosophy. I never quite had the patience for the rigorous thought and logical minutiae that philosophy demands. This book will not reflect the intellectual rigor of the philosopher nor the scientific expertise of the physicist. It is, instead, my story—that of an English major who has grappled with metaphysical questions of consciousness and death for most of her life.

So I did not get a degree in philosophy, but I did the next best thing: marry someone with a doctorate in philosophy. While at Columbia, I met my husband Bob, who was pursuing his MBA after a career in academia as a philosophy professor. He has kept me intellectually honest, in as much as I allow him. After completing my master's degree, I began work as a speech pathologist. Bob and I got married, and we started a family. I was tending my garden.

Two

A Death and A Survival

All truth passes through three stages. First, it is ridiculed. Second, it is violently opposed. Third, it is accepted as being self-evident.

Arthur Schopenhauer

A Death. In 1986, my father was diagnosed with cancer. He passed away in 1991, having lived a productive and meaningful life for most of that time. Although we expected his death, it propelled me into a very strange mental state. I think, in psychological terms, I was having brief episodes of dissociation involving derealization. I remained completely functional, but I would find myself at times looking at the environment, particularly man-made aspects such as buildings, roads, houses, street signs, and lights, and experiencing a feeling that these objects were somehow not real. This went on for several months, and rather than being disturbed by it, I experienced it as an almost spiritual, altered state of consciousness. His passing also rekindled my search for answers about the nature of reality and death.

At the time, I was working in a hospital. There was no internet then, or not that I had access to, but I did have access to the medical library, where I could order copies of articles that interested me. I read everything I could that had to do with near-death experiences (NDEs), including Raymond Moody's groundbreaking *Life After Life*. While exploring the topic of NDEs, I encountered a related topic, out-of-body experiences (OBEs or OOBEs), and I read Robert Monroe's autobiographical *Journeys Out of the Body*. Through the medical library, I found six articles on NDEs in medical journals ranging in date from 1974 to 1986, and I still have the copies. That marked the start of my readings in an attempt to understand life, death, and consciousness.

All in all, the readings on near-death experiences were inconclusive and less than satisfying. The scientific study of NDEs was in its infancy. It was comprised primarily of case studies and anecdotes. Some of these were quite compelling but did not provide proof of an afterlife. The journal articles were written either from the perspective of those sincerely interested in the topic, who leaned towards the belief that NDEs point to an afterlife, or from the perspective of debunkers offering alternative explanations for the phenomenon. It was impossible to determine the truth of the matter. Since that time, a great deal of additional scientific inquiry has been completed, and more is ongoing. Many of the debunkers' alternative explanations have been disputed with success. However, these studies do not rise to the level of proof. (More on this in Chapter Six.) I found my readings intriguing and inspiring, but far from definitive.

Around this time, I also discovered the book *Death and Consciousness,* by David H. Lund, a professor emeritus of philosophy at Bemidji State University in Minnesota. Here he gives compelling reasons for the notion that consciousness may not be a property of the brain, that the brain acts as a receiver rather than a generator of consciousness. He argues that our consciousness, our sense of having subjective experiences, or what the philosophers call *qualia,* is something completely different than the physical material of the world that can be observed and measured.

Lund goes on to show that his non-materialist view is no less cogent than that of the materialist view that consciousness arises from the material of the brain. We see that consciousness fluctuates with brain states, and the materialist may view this as proof that consciousness is a product of the brain. For example, when one has a concussion from a head injury, consciousness is altered. However, the neural correlates of consciousness and brain states are just that—correlates. These correlations of brain state and conscious phenomena are equally consistent with the brain as a receiver of consciousness. To quote the Dalai Lama, "The view that all mental processes are necessarily physical processes is a metaphysical assumption, not a scientific fact" (2006).

The concept of the brain as a receiver of consciousness is not new and goes back to philosopher Henri Bergson (1859–1941). William James (1842–1910), philosopher, psychologist, and one of the darlings of the New

Age movement (along with Carl Jung), further developed this concept in his *transmission theory* of consciousness. A popular analogy, albeit a somewhat mechanistic one, likens consciousness to a television transmission being received when the television is tuned to a specific channel. Here, the brain functions like the television—not generating the program or its content but receiving, decoding, and displaying it. If the television malfunctions, the picture becomes distorted, just as consciousness appears impaired or distorted in the presence of a brain injury. A more recent analogy is that of the computer and the internet. The computer is a receiving and transmitting device, and the internet and its websites remain in existence when the computer is shut down.

Aldous Huxley (1894–1963) famously described the brain as a "reducing valve" in his book *The Doors of Perception* (1954). Ken Kesey (1935–2001) further elaborated in *The Electric Kool-Aid Acid Test* (Wolfe 1968): "[Huxley] compared the brain to a 'reducing valve.' In ordinary perception, the senses send an overwhelming flood of information to the brain, which the brain then filters down to a trickle it can manage for the purpose of survival in a highly competitive world." Your organs of perception take in limited information from the environment and transmit that information to your brain. For instance, human visual and auditory perception can only detect a narrow range of light wavelengths and sound frequencies, respectively, filtering out everything that doesn't serve the purpose of survival. Other species' sense organs see, hear, and smell things we can't but may not be able to perceive things we can, such as color. The brain then interprets this sensory input, further filtering out extraneous information to create a unified interpretation of reality that can be acted upon coherently. Without such filtering, you would be completely overwhelmed and unable to function in any meaningful way.

It has been suggested that savantism is an example of the brain failing to act as a reducing valve, particularly in sudden or acquired savantism (as opposed to developmental savantism usually associated with autism spectrum disorder). In *acquired savant syndrome,* a person suddenly develops a completely new and extraordinary skill following a brain injury such as a concussion, as if the ability has been "downloaded" from a source outside the brain. This skill is often in music, mathematics, or the visual arts and sometimes results in entirely new careers and even public acclaim. In addition, recent medical literature has described a *sudden savant syndrome,* which arises suddenly in a person with no disability or precipitating brain injury (Treffert 2021).

Not only can the brain act as a reducing valve, but the mind can also alter the function of the brain. Support for this comes from the area of dissociative identity disorder (DID), formerly known as multiple personality disorder. Through EEG studies of the brain in persons with DID, it appears that the (immaterial?) mind can change the function of the brain. The case of a patient, B.T., revealed that when she was exhibiting one of her blind personalities, there was a complete absence of visual evoked potentials. When a sighted personality was present, visual evoked potentials were normal (Strasburger and Waldvogel 2015).

Our minds alter the structure and function of our brains in more mundane ways as well. During PET scan imaging, patients have been instructed to think of a particular thing, a rose for example. The patient then decides to think of the rose, and corresponding areas of the brain "light up." Studies show that practicing a skill, such as playing a musical instrument, alters the structure and function of the brain. And the brain scans of long-term meditators show significant differences in structure and function. These appear to be cases of the mind telling the brain what to do. Of course, these brain changes in response to changes in mental activity are all correlates and say nothing about causation or the direction of causation.

Lund further argues that there is evidence from the field of parapsychology that consciousness does act separately from the brain and that it may survive bodily death. I can almost hear your eyes rolling at the mention of parapsychology, and no doubt many of you believe it to be a pseudoscience (a pejorative epithet frequently applied to parapsychology as a means of dismissing it). Actually, parapsychology is a legitimate field of scientific inquiry that studies psychic phenomena, or psi. It applies the scientific method to the examination of a commonly reported human experience. In 1969, the Parapsychological Association became an official affiliate of the American Association for the Advancement of Science, the world's largest scientific organization and the publisher of *Science*, one of the most highly regarded scientific journals.

Over the past century or so, some notable luminaries of science, initially skeptical, weighed in positively regarding the existence of psychic phenomena. In his later writings, Sigmund Freud (1856–1939) noted experiments he had conducted that supported telepathy. Mathematician Alan Turing (1912–1954) stated that while he found the phenomena of ESP disturbing, the statistical evidence was overwhelming. Carl Sagan (1934–1996), a renowned scientist who devoted much of his career to debunking pseudoscience, wrote in *The Demon-Haunted World*:

> Perhaps one percent of the time, someone who has an idea that smells, feels, and looks indistinguishable from the usual run of pseudoscience will turn out to be right. [...] At the time of writing there are three claims in the ESP field which, in my opinion, deserve serious study: (1) that by thought alone humans can (barely) affect random number generators in computers; (2) that people under mild sensory deprivation can receive thoughts or images "projected" at them; and (3) that young children sometimes report the details of a previous life, which upon checking turn out to be accurate and which they could not have known about in any other way than reincarnation. (Sagan 1996, p. 302)

However, Sagan qualified this statement, adding:

> I pick these claims not because I think they're likely to be valid (I don't), but

as examples of contentions that might be true. The last three have at least some, although still dubious, experimental support. Of course, I could be wrong. (Sagan 1996, p. 302)

Faint encouragement indeed. Still, as a founder of the Committee for Skeptical Inquiry (formerly known as CSICOP—the Committee for the Scientific Investigation of Claims of the Paranormal, an organization created for the implicit purpose of discrediting parapsychology—notice the "COP" in CSICOP), the fact that Sagan left the door open to the possibility of psi is remarkable. The taboo against parapsychology within the sciences is so strong that it limits funding and career advancement, generally discourages research and publication, and can stifle legitimate inquiry.

From a statistical standpoint, there is strong support for psi. Jessica Utts is a professor of statistics at the University of California, Irvine, a past president of the American Statistical Association, and the author of several textbooks on statistics. She is also a researcher in parapsychology. In "An Assessment of the Evidence for Psychic Functioning," published in 1995 and republished in 2019, she states:

Using the standards applied to any other area of science, it is concluded that psychic functioning has been well established. The statistical results of the studies examined are far beyond what is expected by chance. Arguments that these results could be due to methodological flaws in the experiments are soundly refuted. [... Results] have been replicated at a number of laboratories across the world. Such consistency cannot be readily explained by claims of flaws or fraud. (Utts 2019)

And in a 2007 web interview for UC Davis, Utts discusses and further underscores the rigorous scientific basis for parapsychology research:

Utts points out that hundreds of tightly controlled, published parapsychology studies meet the rigorous scientific criteria established to weed out flukes and shams. [...] "I think students are surprised by how much research there's been on this subject, and the quality of it," says Utts. [...] However, Utts finds that [...] people's beliefs (or disbeliefs) about parapsychology are often so entrenched that reams of published data are not enough to change their minds. (Parker 2007)

It is the very existence of psychic phenomena that bolsters the concept of the mind or consciousness acting separately from or outside the brain. Psychic phenomena, or psi, include telepathy, remote viewing, clairvoyance, precognition, and mind-matter interaction (also called psychokinesis or telekinesis). Reduced to its most basic aspects, psi is divided into information coming into a person's conscious or subconscious awareness without the perception of the ordinary sense organs, and information going out or being emitted from a person to affect objects at a distance without physical contact. If this were possible, and a substantial body of evidence indicates that it is not only possible but probable, then this would suggest that consciousness acts outside the confines of the brain. While this notion of consciousness as separate from the brain may be necessary for the possibility of survival of bodily death, it is not a sufficient condition to presume survival. This would not prove that individual consciousness survives beyond death, but it would go a long way to making it a possibility.

Fear and Searching in Michigan. There is nothing like a serious illness to reawaken questions of mortality. The hopes and fears also make bias more likely. I try to stay honest with myself. At age thirty-nine, five years after my father's passing, and with two young children at home, I was diagnosed with breast cancer. It appeared to be caught early, and I underwent a lumpectomy, radiation, and six months of chemotherapy. Then I put it all behind me. A year and a half later, the cancer had returned. I then went through a double mastectomy and nine months of chemotherapy. My care at Beaumont Hospital in Michigan was excellent, but with the cancer's return, I felt sure I would die. That was twenty-six years ago. The experience profoundly impacted my outlook on life, much of it in a positive way in the long run.

However, the initial fear was significant. I felt a need to believe in a spiritual reality and a life after death. Not surprisingly, this need could color or alter one's objectivity. This is an objection often cited by skeptics towards parapsychology and studies involving near-death experiences (NDEs) and related phenomena. Many of the scientists involved in such studies can be labeled "true believers," and the debunkers claim that this influences all parapsychological research. On the other side of the equation, the skeptical debunkers are often just as much "true believers" in the Scientific Orthodoxy, such that they also are unable to be unbiased. The need to believe or disbelieve something does not change its ultimate reality. It does make it more difficult to perceive that reality accurately.

So in 1999, having completed my cancer treatments, I embarked on an adventure of reading and pursuing unusual experiences. I remembered my reading of Lund's book *Death and Consciousness* and continued my exploration at the local Barnes & Noble and Borders bookstores. (Ahhh, the pleasures of perusing fully stocked brick-and-mortar bookstores before the rise of online shopping!) There, in the discount section, I discovered three wonderful books: *The Conscious Universe,* by Dean Radin (1997); *Parapsychology, Philosophy, and Spirituality: A Postmodern Exploration,* by David Ray Griffin (SUNY University of New York Press, 1997); and *Unsnarling the World-Knot,* also by David Ray Griffin (University of California Press, 1998).

Dean Radin holds a master's degree in electrical engineering and a PhD in educational psychology from the University of Illinois at Urbana-Champaign. His graduate work was in artificial intelligence and computer models of cognition. He worked on advanced telecommunications systems at Bell Labs, as a researcher at Princeton University and the University of Edinburgh, and was a faculty member at the University of Nevada. He is currently Chief Scientist at the Institute of Noetic Science (IONS) in California. David Ray Griffin (1939–2022) was a professor of philosophy of religion and theology at the Claremont School of Theology and was a proponent of Alfred North Whitehead's Process Philosophy. Unfortunately, in his latter years, he "went off the rails" into 9/11 conspiracy theory, but that should not negate the quality of his earlier work.

Parapsychology, Philosophy, and Spirituality recalled for me themes from Lund's book. As best stated on the back cover of Griffin's *Parapsychology*: "Griffin examines why scientists, philosophers, and theologians have held parapsychology in disdain, and he argues that neither *a priori* philosophical attacks [basing an argument on pre-held assumptions that may or may not be true] nor wholesale rejection of the evidence can withstand scrutiny" (Richard S. Broughton, Director, Institute for Parapsychology, 1997). In his book, Griffin lays out evidence from parapsychology that the mind, or consciousness, is not confined to the brain. It can perceive and act at a distance.

When it comes to explaining the legitimacy of parapsychology and the case for the existence of psi, nobody does it better than Dean Radin. In *The Conscious Universe* and his later works, including *Entangled Minds* (2006), his evidence goes far beyond anecdotes (although many compelling anecdotes are also recounted). He provides a thoroughgoing review of the experimental laboratory research and includes the use of the more recent statistical tool of meta-analysis. He is a master at debunking the debunkers. "Cutting perceptively through the spurious arguments frequently made by skeptics, [Radin] shows the evidence in favor of [paranormal] existence is overwhelming" (Brian Josephson, Nobel laureate in physics and professor of physics, Cambridge University, 1997). He shows that the skeptics' usual suspects of superstition, fraud, chance, methodological flaws, and misinterpretation do not hold up to examination. I will not attempt an exhaustive summary of Radin's work here. Rather, if you are interested, I strongly recommend reading his books in their entirety. Following are some highlights from his work.

Radin shows that laboratory experiments provide statistical evidence for psi with odds against chance routinely ranging from 100 to 1 up to odds in the tens of trillions to one. He describes classes of experiments showing extraordinary evidence, or what would be considered extraordinary in other scientific disciplines. These include experiments in telepathy, remote viewing, presentiment, implicit precognition, and experiments examining the effect of consciousness on random number generators. He states that with these "six classes of experimental protocols that exceed combined odds against chance of 1 billion to 1, [...] there is no need for further proof-oriented scientific evidence," and "that some forms of psi exist—is for all practical purposes settled" (Radin 2018, p. 99).

I mention here several experiments I found particularly interesting. In ganzfeld experiments, a mild form of sensory deprivation is used to produce an altered state. (*Ganzfeld* means "whole field" in German.) Parapsychology experiments have shown that psi is increased during altered states of consciousness. While in this relaxed state, the subject verbalizes their impressions about a target picture or video at a remote location. Sometimes there is a "sender" who is attempting to convey information about the target. These experiments resulted in hit rates of 33 percent, where 25 percent would be expected by chance. A meta-analysis of ganzfeld experiments showed significant results.

Another fascinating type of experiment bypasses reliance on subjective conscious perception entirely (Radin 2006, chap. 7). To test unconscious psi, researchers select pairs of subjects who share a close connection, such as couples, siblings, friends, or even twins. Testing involves the use of galvanic skin response, EEG, or functional magnetic resonance imaging (fMRI). Participants are separated in electromagnetically sealed and soundproofed rooms, and the partners are instructed to try to maintain a mental connection with each other. The "receiving" subject simply relaxes, while the "sending" subject observes the receiver on a computer screen. In some experiments, the sender is randomly instructed to send calming or activating messages to the receiver. In other scenarios, the sender may be activated or stimulated by something like a flashing light or loud noise presented at random. Results show a highly significant correlation in responses between partners, where the receiving partner's skin or brain reacted when the sending partner was sending activating messages or being stimulated by flashes of light. These experiments have been replicated by independent researchers.

Similarly interesting studies looked at subconscious or unconscious presentiment (precognition, or "telling the future"). According to Radin, "It appears that our nervous system can perceive about five seconds into the future" (Radin 2004). Using electrical skin resistance to measure sweat gland activity, a subject presses a button, and after five seconds a computer displays either a calm or emotionally charged photo at random. There is a rest period, and then the process repeats for a duration of about thirty minutes. On average, subjects' nervous systems respond about five seconds *before* the stimulus is presented. These studies have been replicated by independent researchers, and some have included measures of heart rate and brain activity as well as skin response. Does this unconscious presentiment provide an evolutionary advantage? Perhaps, without being consciously aware of it, we use presentiment in our everyday lives.

Mind-matter interaction may also operate both consciously and unconsciously. The Princeton Engineering Anomalies Research Laboratory (PEAR Lab) conducted and published numerous studies showing that it is possible to mentally influence the outcomes of random number generators (RNGs). An RNG is an advanced technological version of a coin flip or dice throw that eliminates possible unintended noise in the data. Field-consciousness experiments take advantage of this use of RNGs to explore the effect of focused group energy on the physical environment, looking for increased coherence in output deviating from expected output reflective of the RNG's usual randomness (Radin 2006).

Among the most intriguing of these is the Global Consciousness Project. The GCP is a network of RNGs on computers spread throughout six continents. Each computer continually collects samples of 200 random bits per second while they all "wait" for something to happen. Something did happen—on September 11, 2001, the day of the attacks on the World Trade Center. On that day, the normal bell curve of expected RNG recordings deviated markedly from what would be expected. Similar deviations, but to a lesser degree, have been observed for the funeral of Princess Diana and for the Indonesian tsunami of 2004.

I want to note here the skeptics' often-quoted trope, "Extraordinary claims require extraordinary evidence," first popularized by Carl Sagan. What does this actually mean? In the skeptical literature, extraordinary evidence is an always-moving target. Statistician Jessica Utts describes a collaboration that took place in 1986 between esteemed psychologist and parapsychologist Charles Honorton (1946–1992) and Ray Hyman, professor emeritus of psychology at the University of Oregon and a noted critic of parapsychology:

> [They] devoted eight pages to "Recommendations for Future Psi Experiments," careful-

ly outlining details for how the experiments should be conducted and reported. Honorton and his colleagues then conducted several hundred trials using these specific criteria and found essentially the same effect sizes as in earlier work [...]. I would expect Professor Hyman to be very interested in the results of these experiments he helped to create. While he did acknowledge that they "have produced intriguing results," it is both surprising and disappointing that he spent only a scant two paragraphs at the end of his discussion on these results. Instead, Hyman seems to be proposing yet another set of requirements to be satisfied before parapsychology should be taken seriously. It is difficult to sort out what those requirements should be from his account. (Utts 1991)

Theories that fall within the current physicalist paradigm, such as string theory, multiple dimensions, the multiverse, and many theories within the "soft sciences" of psychology and medicine, are readily entertained with much less than the extreme level of extraordinary evidence demonstrated in more than a century of parapsychological research.

One of the criticisms often leveled at parapsychology is that the results are weak or trivial. Although the demonstrated combined odds against chance are very high, the effects observed in experiments are often small—for example, a hit rate of 54 percent, when 50 percent would be expected by chance. The possible reasons for this are many. This 54 percent is similar to the results of much research in psychology and the so-called "soft sciences," where experiments look at human and animal abilities, behaviors, and interactions. Also, psychic perceptions generally compete with more obvious perceptions coming in through the ordinary five senses. And according to parapsychologists, "talent" for psi is distributed among humans along a normal bell curve. Some individuals show a much stronger ability than others, and much of the research has been conducted on those with no exceptional talent.

Then there is the issue of saliency. Psi appears to be shy and does not shine in controlled laboratory settings, as it does spontaneously when the outcome is meaningful to the individual. Spontaneous incidents of psi can be dramatic but are relegated to the category of anecdote. Finally, there are the usual questions—"Why don't psychics clean up at the casino?" (Because, even if they have a slight advantage, the odds are always in the house's favor, regardless.) "Why can't you (the psychic) tell me (this, that, or the other thing)?" "Why were you wrong about...?" And, of course, there are the comedic bits, such as Steven Wright's, "All those who believe in psychokinesis, raise my hand." It just doesn't work that way.

Three

Black Swans and White Crows

There are things known and things unknown,
and in between are the doors of perception.
Aldous Huxley

So at this point in my seeking, I'm fairly convinced about psi, but not that it provides definitive evidence for survival beyond death (the survival hypothesis). In addition, when you peruse the internet and read dozens of pages on parapsychology, you find conflicting information about the experimental evidence for psi. I realize that mathematics has never been my strongest suit, and I've never taken a formal class in statistics, so I may not be the best judge. When it comes to whether science supports the reality of psychic phenomena and you read the experts on both sides, it begins to sound a lot like, "No, it doesn't. Yes, it does. No, it doesn't. Yes, it does. No, it doesn't. Yes, it does."

Not to worry. In an address given to the Joint Statistical Meetings in Chicago, Jessica Utts stated, "When I have given talks on this topic [of psi] to audiences of statisticians, I show lots of data. Then I ask the audience, which would be more convincing to you—lots more data, or one strong personal experience? Almost without fail, the response is one strong personal experience" (Utts 2016).

In a related vein, the Harvard psychologist and philosopher William James is frequently quoted: "If you wish to upset the law that all crows are black, you mustn't seek to show that no crows are; it is enough if you prove one single crow to be white." He wrote this regarding his search for a true psychic medium. For James, that "white crow" was Leonora Piper (1857–1950). He stated, "In the trances of this medium, I cannot resist the conviction that knowledge appears which she has never gained by the ordinary waking use of her eyes and ears and wits." He may have derived his inspiration for his white crow from the "black swan" taken originally from the second-century Roman poet Juvenal's "a bird as rare upon the earth as a black swan." At that time, black swans were thought not to exist. The phrase "black swan" became common in 16th-century England to indicate something that was impossible. Then in the 17th century, Dutch explorers discovered actual black swans in Australia. From that time forward, "black swan" would connote a form of logical fallacy.

But in terms of psychic phenomena, what would qualify as a white crow? Would an anecdote suffice? Could one perceive something as a white crow, but it would really be a trick of the light, something seen from a distance, or even self-delusion? I decided it was time to seek my own black swan/white crow personal experience and decide for myself. I would be seeking the White Crow.

By its very nature, this personal white crow would be anecdotal to others. It likely wouldn't carry much weight, particularly with strangers and casual acquaintances. I recall reading that, much like believing personal experience over statistics, people tend to believe and be swayed by the experiences of close friends and family members (Markovsky and Thye 2021). This is in our nature as social animals, and it creates social cohesion and an evolutionary advantage. As I embarked on my search for the white crow, I encountered stories of personal experiences shared by friends. I will begin the tale of my quest by recounting several of these.

Our family belonged to a Humanistic Jewish organization, the Jewish Parents Institute (JPI), where we developed close friendships, and our children attended Sunday school. One evening a friend, Lynn, told me about her mother who could see auras around people and could reliably tell when someone was going to die in the near future. Peggy, another friend from JPI, shared a story about an incident that happened before mobile phones were commonplace. Her mother had sent her father to the store to pick up some things. He was driving home when a sudden, very clear message popped into his mind—"Go back; you have to buy vacuum bags." When he returned home with them, he said to his wife, "Honey, don't do that to me again." Mundane, but interesting.

A third incident was relayed to me by another friend, Nikki, with whom I had spoken about my metaphysical quest. She had been practicing astral projection, or out-of-body experiences, for years. She told me about one of her first experiences from her college years. While "out of body," she found herself in front of her grandmother's house, walked up the steps, and passed right through the closed front door. She noticed large, white, puffy things on her grandmother's feet and thought, "Those are strange slippers." Nikki's aunt had also been present in the house. The next day, Nikki asked her mother how her grandmother was. She was told that her grandmother had just had surgery on her feet to remove bunions, that her feet had been bandaged, and that Nikki's aunt was staying with her grandmother.

Intriguing, but I needed to seek my own experiences. How would I go about that? Well, I took classes in meditation, psychic development, and Reiki. I kept a dream journal. I read everything I could about out-of-body experiences and began working towards having one. I also had a massage therapist who became a friend. She was a practicing Wiccan, and she invited me to join her small coven. Yup, I joined a Wiccan coven.

If the parapsychologists are correct and psychic ability is distributed along a bell curve, then I am probably on the lower end of that curve. In my Reiki classes, I definitely could **not** "feel energy." It felt like make-believe. The Wiccan rituals I attended were fun, but I never felt like I truly belonged. Also, still make-believe. I had greater success with psychic development and with out-of-body exploration. What follows are my personal anecdotes.

The first of these took place about twenty-five years ago during a psychic development class. We were learning intuitive billet reading—yes, like the sealed envelope trick lampooned by Johnny Carson playing his comedic character "Carnac the Magnificent" on *The Tonight Show* in the 1960s. In class, we each wrote a question, sealed it in an envelope, and placed it in a bowl. We took turns selecting an envelope and voicing whatever impressions came to mind as we held it. Then the envelope was opened, and the question was read aloud.

I remember making up whatever story came to me in the moment. I said that a man was worried about money and supporting his family. He had lost his job and was trying to start his own business. This venture was not working out as he had hoped. Eventually, he would return to a job similar to his previous one but would continue the new business as a sideline.

The actual situation was essentially identical, except that the final outcome was unknown. This question had been written by a woman whose husband had lost his job. He was developing a new business and was self-employed. She wanted to know how it would turn out. For my part, I did not have any visions, hear any whisperings in my ear, or have any uncanny sense of knowing. I simply made up a story that came to me as I held the sealed envelope.

Recently, I had similar experiences during a psychic workshop where we explored psychometry—divining facts about an object, or a person associated with it, by holding the object. I held a locket, and I stated that it had belonged to a teenage girl with long, dark, straight hair parted in the middle, dressed in jeans and a dark t-shirt. She thought she was cool or tough, but she wore the locket hidden beneath her clothes, and it held a special meaning for her. It was revealed that these observations were all correct and referred to one of the participants at a much younger age. (Currently, the woman did not have dark, straight hair and did not resemble the description at all.)

In the same workshop, I held a Santa necklace. I described a little girl with baby-fine blond hair, wearing a dress. She appeared to be around two years old. I stated that she was holding the necklace and squatting, the way young children do, by a Christmas tree. I also noted that the necklace did not belong to the little girl. Again, these observations were all correct, and the woman in question did not currently have fine, blond hair. Whether my impressions were influenced by visual cues from the objects themselves, whether the women confirmed information that was not strictly true due to bias within the context of the exercise, or whether I was sensing the information psychically, I cannot say. I've since contacted the women to verify the details, and they confirmed the information was correct.

In the late 2000s, I was visiting colleges with my youngest daughter. We stayed at a bed and breakfast in Ohio that was purported to be haunted. The food was good, but the facility was in poor repair, and nothing worked properly in our first room. We switched rooms, and the second room was marginally better, so we just stayed there and put up with it. When we checked out the following morning, we were told that we had stayed in one of the most haunted rooms. We had no experiences during the night that would suggest this. However, when we went out to our car to head home, my seat had been drastically moved, slid all the way back and reclined in such a way that I would have been unable to drive. My daughter said, "Oh, Mom, you must have bumped something when we were getting our suitcases." I don't see how this could have happened, and nothing similar had occurred before or has happened since.

Approximately ten years ago, I attended a small gathering at the home of a local psychic medium here in Maryland who was supposedly delivering messages from the dead. She went around the circle, speaking to each of us in turn. To my ears, the messages seemed quite generic but appeared meaningful to the recipients. When she came to me, she said, "I have a message from someone with a long 'ee' in their name." "Could it be Sophie or Molly, my grandmothers?" I asked. She replied that no, the long "ee" sound was the main part of the name—the primary syllable—and said she would come back to me. I had no idea who she was talking about. When she came back around the circle, she said the message was that I needed to apologize. Immediately, I thought of my mother-in-law, Lee, who had not been in my conscious thoughts at all. She and I did not get along, and I was not kind to her. I was probably a bit of a jerk. Apparently, she is still haunting me.

Several incidents that could be characterized as psychic or paranormal occurred at the end of my mother's life. The last few weeks, when she was in at-home hospice care, and then the weeks following, when I was managing her house and estate, were especially fraught. I stayed with my mother at her house through much of her final month. On October 6th of that year, in the early morning hours while at my mother's house, I had an unusually vivid dream. I dreamed that female firefighters were putting out a large fire. They discovered black mold, and they transformed into construction contractors. They were breaking down walls, removing siding and beams, exposing posts, and disrupting our lives. I asked one young female worker how long it would take. She looked into my eyes and asked, "How long do you think it will take?" I said, "Thirty days." Still looking at me directly, she said pointedly, "Nineteen days." My mother passed away not on the nineteenth day, but thirteen days later on the 19th of the month. I wrapped things up at the house on the 24th, the nineteenth day, and headed home.

Another incident occurred several weeks after my mother's death. I had decided to attempt managing her estate without the assistance of a lawyer, as I was not working and had the time. I stayed in her house for a few days to deal with local bank accounts, insurance brokers, auction houses, and the like. On the morning that I was to drive to the county courthouse probate office, something impelled me to go into my mother's closet and put on one of her sweaters. I also put my father's dog tags on my keychain. I was anxious that all would go smoothly and there would be no nasty and costly surprises. When I went through security at the courthouse, the officer noticed the dog tags. He was a veteran and reacted warmly with pleasant comments. Then, as I sat down with the Register of Wills, the first thing she said was, "I have that same sweater. It's one of my favorites." It set a very positive tone for the meeting, and she was extremely helpful.

During much of my time seeking white crows, I focused on reading about and attempting to have out-of-body experiences (OBEs), such as those I remembered from my early childhood. I began this practice in the second half of 1999, approximately twenty-five years ago, and have continued intermittently since then with periods of practice and long hiatuses. I read numerous books on out-of-body experiences—revisiting Robert Monroe's classic *Journeys Out of the Body* and reading others for the first time, such as William Buhlman's widely known *Adventures Beyond the Body*. I also read instruction manuals for achieving astral projection and listened to audio recordings designed to induce OBEs.

In the OBE literature, experiencers express no doubt that the experiences are real and not dreams. They generally describe their out-of-body experiences as extremely vivid and "more real than real." They report lifting or rolling out of their bodies and exploring astral facsimiles of the physical world and other astral planes. Often before "separating" from their bodies, they have a sensation of vibrating, known as the vibrational state. They recount veridical experiences in which they see something while projecting, which they later verify as real. The experience of my friend Nikki, described earlier, is an example.

Personally, I experienced nothing so dramatic. I experimented with various techniques as I was going to sleep at night or if I awakened in the middle of the night or early morning hours. I found the methods described in Buhlman's book to be the most helpful. The trick is to leverage the state between sleeping and waking and to somehow keep your mind awake as your body falls asleep, which puts you in an altered state of consciousness. I had several unusual experiences but always felt afterwards that they could have been dreams. Here are some entries from my journals:

September 24, 1999 — In a hypnogogic state (somewhere between asleep and awake), I will myself out of body and stand on the floor beside my bed. I then float down the hall into the living room to look around, but I can't see. I open my astral eyes and begin to see dimly. I float around for a bit, then want to return to my body. I float back to my room and look down at myself lying next to my husband. I will myself back into my body but feel as though I'm not fitting quite right. I tell myself to go to sleep and that I will settle in as I sleep. The next morning, I remember the experience, though it feels as if it could have been a dream.

October 15, 2020 — As I'm falling asleep, I feel mild vibrations. I sit up halfway out of my body, but cannot move beyond. I stay there for a short while, then lie back down and return to sleep.

May 20, 2021 — I awaken in the early morning hours and practice a technique. I feel mild vibrations. I sit up out of my body but move sluggishly and feel heavy. Somehow, I end up on the floor in a ball at the foot of my bed. I push myself up and can see dimly. I then awaken in bed.

September 12, 2021 — At approximately 7 a.m., I awaken after a full night's sleep. I fall back asleep and say to my self in my sleep, "Oh, this is ridiculous. I'm just going to do it. Out of Body Now!" I find myself out of my body, feeling slow, sluggish, and without sight. I say, "Door Now!" and move to the bedroom door. I then say to myself, "Front Door Now!" and "Through Door!" and feel myself moving through the closed door (like a ghost). I still have no vision and say, "Clarity Now!" Then I am standing outside, examining the leaves of an evergreen in detail. I see a small group of high-school-age girls on the street (unlikely, because it was a Sunday, and teens would probably still be sleeping). I continue to "fly" around them in a swimming motion. Then I am asleep. When I awaken, it feels like it may have been a dream.

May 2, 2023 — It's 4 a.m., and I am lying in bed, alert, after having slept approximately four and a half hours. I am relaxed and focused, and I hear several pings and zings over several minutes. This is not terribly unusual for me. I sometimes hear sounds as I fall asleep. In my mind, I state, "Out of body now!" I feel very pronounced vibrations moving up and down my body, and this is quite unusual. In fact, it's the first time I've felt the vibrations so strongly. I attempt to allow the vibrations to peak and try to will myself out of my body, but nothing happens.

So what does this all mean? Has it proved anything? Does it move me forward in my quest? Does it say anything about the reality of psychic phenomena or the possibility or reality of life after death? It may say very little, at least about survival of consciousness beyond bodily death. My fledgling out-of-body experiences that occurred while I was in an altered state felt quite dream-like and say nothing substantial. My experiences do not seem to be equivalent to those described by some, and I had no veridical experiences.

Even if I had had a dramatic, veridical out-of-body experience, it would only go so far in moving the needle towards the possibility of an afterlife. (More about this in Chapter Six.) What about the psychic experiences, especially the billet reading and psychometry? I must admit, those experiences, along with the scientific literature, convince me that, as Dean Radin would say, "There is something interesting going on." But what is that interesting something? What does it say about the nature of reality, of consciousness, and of the possibility of personal survival beyond death? To explore this, I venture into the realms of physics and philosophy.

Four

Psi and Psi

I regard consciousness as fundamental. I regard matter as derivative from consciousness. We cannot get behind consciousness. Everything that we talk about, everything that we regard as existing, postulates consciousness.

Max Planck, originator of quantum theory

Soon after my father's passing, as part of my search for deeper meaning, I turned to readings on quantum mechanics. I had learned nothing about quantum physics in high school in the '70s, and quantum theory was certainly not available in high school textbooks. (It is currently being introduced in advanced high school physics courses.) Among my father's books, I discovered *The Tao of Physics*, by Fritjof Capra (1975). This best-selling classic explores the parallels between modern physics and Eastern religion. Another illuminating book I encountered was *In Search of Schrödinger's Cat: Quantum Physics and*

Reality, by John Gribbin (1984). If it seems there is a great deal of reading in my quest, that is because reading is one of the primary ways I process and make sense of the world. I hope that I'm pulling the information together in new ways.

The New Age movement loves to claim that quantum mechanics refutes materialism, supports New Age mysticism, and bolsters concepts such as "We create our own reality." On the other hand, most traditional physicists cry foul, stating that there is absolutely no relationship between quantum physics and mysticism, that quantum mechanics has been misappropriated, and that the New Agers have no idea what they are talking about. For their part, those with a mystical bent widely quote some of the venerable early originators and developers of quantum theory who expressed mystical leanings. These physicists included Heisenberg, Schrodinger, de Broglie, Jeans, Planck, Pauli, Eddington, Wigner, and Wheeler. An example is Max Planck's 1931 statement to *The Observer* (London), quoted above. Ironically, in the 1960s and '70s, physicists who wanted to explore the deeper meaning and implications of quantum theory were subject to the same sorts of taboos experienced by parapsychologists. Their research funding, publishing opportunities, and job prospects dried up, and some of them hid their philosophical interests and pursued them in secret on the side.

The Nobel laureate physicist Richard Feynman (1918–1988) famously said in his 1964 MIT Messenger Lectures:

I can safely say that nobody understands
quantum mechanics. [...] I am going to tell
you what nature behaves like. If you will
simply admit that maybe she does behave
like this, you will find her a delightful, en-
trancing thing. Do not keep saying to yourself, if you can possibly avoid it, "But how
can it be like that?" because you will get
"down the drain" into a blind alley from
which nobody has yet escaped. Nobody
knows how it can be like that. (Feynman
1965, p. 129)

Perhaps quantum mechanics is so mystifying because
it is counterintuitive and flies in the face of both logic and
common sense. I will not pretend to truly understand the
quantum physics that I'll be discussing in this section,
but I will say that it goes a long way towards providing
a theoretical framework for psychic phenomena.

Let's take a look at the connection between quantum
physics, consciousness, and psychic phenomena (psi). In
physics, Ψ, or psi (pronounced "sigh"), is the Greek sym-
bol for a wave function. Remarkably, physical reality can
be described in mathematical terms as a wave function.
Physical reality is frequently referred to by philosophers
as "the furniture of the universe," and according to physicists, it is made up of quantum particles. But what are
particles?

In his 1924 thesis, Louis de Broglie (1892–1987) was the
first to formally propose wave-particle duality in mat-

ter. He proved, mathematically, that subatomic particles, such as electrons, behave like waves. With $E = mc^2$, Einstein showed that mass (or matter) and energy are equivalent. With $E = hv$ (where v is pronounced "nu"), Planck showed that light energy is quantized, with each particle of light carrying energy hv. Here, h represents Planck's constant, and v ("nu") is a measure of frequency. Only waves have a frequency. De Broglie extended these ideas to suggest that if $E = hv$ applies to light, then matter also has wave-like properties. But a wave in what?

In classical physics, waves occur in a medium such as water or air. In quantum physics, the wave is mathematical or statistical. It is a wave in a mathematical or statistical field. What does that mean in physical terms? What exactly is a field? Who knows? A field is essentially a mathematical function. Then is the physical universe essentially a mathematical wave function? As the physicist Niels Bohr said, "Everything we call real is made of things that cannot be regarded as real. If quantum mechanics hasn't profoundly shocked you, you haven't understood it yet." Or as my grandfather would have said, "So *Nu?!* Who knew?" (*Nu*—in Yiddish, an exclamation of surprise, emphasis, doubt, etc., a statement of "go on... .")

Recently, some scientists have suggested that mathematics or information may provide the basic building blocks of the universe. Physicist Max Tegmark of MIT has proposed that the universe *is* an abstract mathematical structure. Physicist Anton Zeilinger from the University of Vienna has described the universe as being composed of information (Radin 2018). Is the universe a mathematical construct, a logical system that examines relations between abstract concepts? Does this imply that the universe could be a mental construct?

Physicists who take exception to "quantum woo" explain that quantum physics is merely an abstract mathematical tool that describes the probabilities of where a particle might be found in space and time. It says nothing about the nature of reality. This raises the question of whether science is even an appropriate tool for exploring reality. In Buddhism, it is claimed that consciousness is better examined from the inside through first-person contemplative exploration, with such tools as meditation, to understand the deeper nature of reality.

Skeptics claim that psi violates the "laws of nature." They also claim that there is no "theory of psi" that underpins parapsychology. In point of fact, with the recent developments in physics, psi does not violate any laws of science. Furthermore, there are many scientific fields that do not have an agreed-upon overarching theoretical framework. The attempt to seek a connection between quantum physics and psychic phenomena, consciousness, or mysticism has been called a "quantum flapdoodle" by Michael Shermer and other skeptics (a phrase coined by physicist Murray Gell-Mann [1929–2019] to describe the ascription of quantum physics to other subjects). However, as one delves more deeply into quantum theory, parallels between quantum physics and psi become clear. Could quantum theory provide the theoretical framework for parapsychology?

In the philosophy of science, the concept of *consilience* was developed by scientist and philosopher William Whewell (1794–1866) to describe a principle for evaluating the acceptability of a scientific theory. According to the principle of consilience, "Most successful theories in the history of science shared a common property, unifying our picture of the universe. Successful theories were not only able to account for phenomena they were designed to explain but could also be used to explain other areas of study" (Gimbel 2020, p. 100). I think we'll find there is a great deal of consilience between quantum physics and parapsychology.

Quantum Weirdness. Quantum physics is widely referred to as "weird" in both popular and scientific writings. Mainstream scientists object to attempts at connecting the strangeness of the quantum world with "coincidental" similarities in psi. But, as Dean Radin points out, "The fabric of reality suggested by quantum theory and the observations associated with psychic phenomena bear striking resemblances. They are eerily weird in precisely the right way to suggest a meaningful relationship" (Radin 2006, p. 6).

Most relevant to the discussion of consciousness and psi are wave-particle duality and nonlocality/entanglement. Early experiments showing wave-particle duality used photons, but the same effects are seen with electrons, one of the "building blocks" of the physical universe. More recent experiments are beginning to see these effects with larger objects. Essentially, subatomic particles are neither wave nor particle until they are measured. How one decides to measure them determines the outcome. Sometimes they act like particles, and sometimes they act like waves, depending entirely on the setup of the experiment, suggesting to some that conscious observation, or consciousness itself, alters the physical reality of the particle. Others propose that interactions between a wave-particle and its environment cause the collapse of the wave function, thereby creating macroscopic reality. This process, known as *decoherence,* may be involved in a quantum system's interaction with a measuring apparatus—no consciousness required. Still others deny that decoherence solves the "measurement problem."

The first double-slit experiments in the 1800s proved that light was a wave. In the 1920s, double-slit experiments showed that light is both a wave and a particle. In a double-slit experiment, an individual particle is sent through either one slit or two slits. When particles are sent one at a time through a single slit, they create a scatter pattern indicative of their particle-like nature. When sent through two slits, even if they are sent through singly, one at a time, they create an interference or wave pattern, as if each particle goes through both slits simultaneously and is interfering with itself. Which result is obtained is dependent on how the measurement is made. If one tries to determine "which slit" a particle passes through, the interference pattern disappears. When we observe the particles going through one slit or the other, they create a scatter pattern. When we do not, they create a wave pattern. Until the particle is observed, it is neither wave nor particle.

In delayed-choice experiments, first proposed by Princeton physicist John Wheeler (1911–2008), the measurement decision is made *after* the particle leaves its source and *after* it has supposedly gone through one slit or two. The results continue to show that the way it is measured, even after the fact, affects whether the particle is expressed as a wave or a particle. This suggests that which way the particle expresses itself depends on a decision made after it is emitted from its source and even after it has traversed the slit or slits. The act of measurement interacting with the particle causes a change in its original state—how a particle is measured or observed changes its previous behavior retroactively.

Not only does this raise questions of how the mind or consciousness participates in creating reality, but it also speaks to the fluidity of time. It is reminiscent of the parapsychology experiments showing that subjects react unconsciously or somatically before an event (see remarks on presentiment and unconscious psi in Chapter Two). In physics, equations are time-reversible and indicate no direction of time, so the mathematics of physics allows for retrocausation.

Interestingly, similar effects have been seen in neuroscience experiments. In these experiments, a subject's brain activity is monitored in an fMRI scanner while the subject is asked to make a choice. These choices have included the choice to lift or not lift a finger, move or not move a hand, choose between two visual patterns, and the like. The fMRI scans indicate that the brain reacts up to ten seconds before the subject is aware of having made a choice (Soon 2008). Some scientists and philosophers have gone as far as to claim that this shows humans do not have free will in the choices they make. I suggest that another explanation would be that our consciousness may be operating according to quantum principles and is somehow "spread out" in space-time. This would make sense, in that quantum principles underlie all physical reality. And it may be that the random statistical nature of quantum processes somehow allows for free will. In addition, it coincides with our common-sense, everyday experience of being able to make conscious choices, at least about some things.

Quantum entanglement is what Einstein referred to as "spooky action at a distance" when he denied some of the implications of quantum theory. "Spooky action at a distance" is also exactly what we see in telepathy and other forms of psi. When two particles become connected in some way by an event and then are separated, even by vast distances, what happens to one particle immediately affects what happens to the other, such that a measurement on one will determine the measurement of the other. This is irrespective of distance and appears to violate the speed of light. It's as if the particles communicate with each other instantaneously.

Einstein could not accept this, and he, along with Boris Podolsky and Nathan Rosen in their 1935 paper (which became known as the EPR paper), posited the existence of hidden variables that were associated with the separated particles at the point of their becoming entangled. John Bell (1928–1990) developed a theorem to examine the possibility of hidden variables accounting for the "spooky action at a distance." Bell's theorem rests on a combination of logical reasoning and statistical analysis of correlations between measurements, showing that the predictions of quantum mechanics are incompatible with local hidden variable theories of classical physics. This was ultimately put to the test experimentally by Alain Aspect in 1982, and it was proved that, indeed, there were no hidden variables, and quantum entanglement was upheld. Numerous articles and book chapters describe Bell's theorem and Aspect's experiments, and I admit that I find some of the technical specifics (especially those involving mathematics) difficult to grasp.

The entanglement experiments go something like this: Two particles are associated with each other in an apparatus. They could be photons, electrons, or some other subatomic particle. They are then simultaneously emitted in opposite directions, and one of their properties is measured—either spin, polarization, or another property of particles. Instantaneously, the measured value of one of the particles determines the value of the other. For instance, if one is measured to be "spin up," the other will be "spin down," even if they are separated by many miles.

This is as if two best friends, say Harry and Sally, are in separate cities. They both like turkey and pastrami sandwiches equally. When ordering at a deli, they do not communicate by phone, text, etc. Yet every time Harry orders pastrami, Sally orders turkey, and vice versa. However, it is not correct to say that the particles (or Harry and Sally) "communicate" faster than the speed of light, violating known laws of physics. A more recent interpretation is that they remain one entangled unit, in a sense one thing not separated by space or time. They have no definite location until they are measured. Hence, the term often applied to this phenomenon is nonlocality. This might be a stretch in the case of Harry and Sally, but it would be as if their minds were entangled on some level. Recently, experiments have even begun to demonstrate entanglement with larger objects such as molecules and cells, and even some macroscopic objects. While not a mainstream position, some physicists have proposed the holistic concept that the entire universe became entangled at the Big Bang.

What does all this say about psi? Dean Radin states, "Quantum theory and a vast body of supporting experiments tell us that something unaccounted for is connecting otherwise isolated objects. And this is precisely what psi experiences and experiments are telling us" (Radin 2006, p. 231). Nobel laureate physicist and mathematician Sir Roger Penrose is one of the first to have proposed that quantum effects operate within the brain, and according to Radin, psi may be the human experience of quantum entanglement (2006, p. 232).

At this point, given the accepted scientific validity of quantum theory, it is possible to interpret psychic phenomena from a scientific, physicalist framework. This is not your grandfather's materialism; it can more properly be called physicalism. Materialism, in philosophy, suggests that everything is composed of matter, while physicalism encompasses other concepts such as forces, energy, mathematics, space, time, and the laws of quantum mechanics.

Then does quantum mechanics tell us anything about the true nature of reality and consciousness? Perhaps not very much. The laws of physics comprise rules and equations that describe mathematical relationships. Scientist and philosopher Sir Arthur Eddington (1882–1944) stated in *The Nature of the Physical World* (1929), "Our best description of the atom boils down to 'something unknown is doing we don't know what.'" We do know more now, but much mystery persists. As philosopher Philip Goff explains in his excellent and thought-provoking book *Galileo's Error* (2019), the physical sciences tell us "only about causal relationships, about what physical things do," not why they behave that way or what they are. For that, I turn to philosophy.

Five

Flavors of Reality

"Tell me one last thing," said Harry. "Is this real? Or has this been happening inside my head?" Dumbledore beamed at him, [...] "Of course it is happening inside your head, Harry, but why on earth should that mean that it is not real?"
—from *Harry Potter and the Deathly Hallows*
J.K. Rowling

Metaphysics is the branch of philosophy that examines the fundamental nature of reality. You won't find this metaphysics in the New Age section of your local bookstore. Philosophical theories of reality have gone in and out of favor, changing significantly throughout history. Many individual philosophers are known to have revised their own conceptions of reality as their thinking evolved during their lifetimes. What philosophers call the mind-body problem has everything to do with the possibility of an afterlife. The mind-body problem concerns the relationship between the mind, or consciousness, and the body—what they are and how they relate or interact. How you think of this issue impacts whether you can believe that survival beyond death is even possible.

Philosophers answer the mind-body problem with three very different theories: dualism, materialistic monism, and, rising in popularity, panpsychism (which is itself a form of monism). Monism states that the world is made up of only one kind of thing, so the mind and body are of one substance. Dualism contends that mind and body are fundamentally different kinds of things.

These conceptions of reality come in numerous varieties—or "flavors," if you will. On the mind-body menu are: religious dualism, naturalistic dualism, quantum dualism, substance dualism, property dualism, object monism, property monism, substance monism, dual aspect monism, pluralistic monism, neutral monism, pan-experientialism, pancognitivism, cosmopsychism, and panprotopsychism. That is not an exhaustive list, and it doesn't even include pantheism or panentheism, which are theistic views related to panpsychism.

Each of these isms has its own issues that cause philosophers from other isms to reject them. You can see how a person could become frustrated with the ability of philosophy to provide answers. Indeed, philosophers do not claim certainty. "Certainty" would be the province of religion and faith. As my husband likes to say, a jury of philosophers would never convict anyone beyond a reasonable doubt.

So what is consciousness? And what is it that may survive beyond the body (which is not the same question and may have a different answer)? There are a number of ways to define consciousness. One way philosophers describe consciousness is as awareness or the subjective experience of, well, experience—thoughts and emotions, pains and pleasures. It is the taste of cinnamon, the smell of flowers, the redness of an apple, the pain of bumping your toe, the cacophony of a schoolyard at recess. It is also a frisson of fear, pangs of love, and your thoughts as you read these words. It generally does not refer to personality or to self-awareness or self-consciousness. In his famous paper, "What Is It Like to Be a Bat?" (1974), philosopher Thomas Nagel argues that it is subjective experience that defines consciousness. We do not know the subjective experience of navigating our environment by echolocation as a bat does. For Nagel, *what it is like to be* is what defines consciousness.

As I mentioned, there are currently three major approaches to the mind-body problem. These are dualism (subcategorized into property dualism and substance dualism), materialist monism, and panpsychist monism. Prior to the Scientific Revolution of the 16th and 17th centuries, the prevailing conception of reality was an implicit dualism within Western Christianity. The mind, or soul, and the body were separate, yet all were imbued with mystical enchantment and unified under the concept of God. Clearly, this form of dualism implies immortality/survival of bodily death.

It was Galileo Galilei (1564–1642) who divorced considerations of consciousness (or soul?) from the physical sciences entirely. Science was concerned only with what could be described mathematically. Objects only had shape, size, weight, location, motion. They no longer had sensory qualities—taste, smell, color, sound. Matter was within the purview of science, and qualia (the subjective or qualitative properties of experiences) were within the purview of religion. Consciousness could not be observed. For Galileo, who was steeped in Christian thought, these subjective qualities resided within the soul.

What Galileo did for science, René Descartes (1596–1650) did for philosophy and the direction of modern thought for the foreseeable future. He formalized the concept of dualism, which began with his famous "I think, therefore I am." Descartes was a brilliant mathematician and philosopher and is considered the father of modern philosophy. What he was saying in this famous quote is that he knows he exists because he is aware of his own thoughts, his own consciousness. That is the only thing he can be completely sure of.

Descartes went on to reason that the mind and the body are two distinct substances: the material body and the immaterial soul. So early dualism, and the idea that science deals only with the material aspects of existence, arose out of Christian concepts of body and soul. Even today, from a materialist viewpoint, we must acknowledge that everything we perceive is mediated by the senses and the brain. We cannot know anything directly without it going through the gateway of the senses and mind.

From its inception, dualism met with several problems. Philosophers most often cited the interaction problem. How could two vastly different substances interact? How could an immaterial mind cause a material body to move, and how could a material organ, such as the eyes, cause the mind to perceive its environment? For many of the early dualists, the answer was that God somehow caused the interaction.

As science progressed and met with continuing success in describing the physical world, most scientists and philosophers came to embrace materialist monism. That is the view that reality is made up of only one kind of thing, and that thing is material. They rejected the concept of consciousness as a separate entity, and the prevailing view became that consciousness could be fully explained as a part of the material world. So the early Christian dualists, like Galileo, separated consciousness from science, and science then reduced consciousness to the purely material.

Materialism remains the predominant philosophical and scientific paradigm today, but not without contenders, and it does have its own set of issues. In Chapter Three of *Galileo's Error*, Philip Goff asks, "Can physical science explain consciousness?" He answers with a resounding "No," arguing that materialist explanations of consciousness involve an inherent self-contradiction. (Although, who's to say that contradiction is even a problem, given that conventional logic does not hold for quantum mechanics, where something can be both wave and particle simultaneously? But I digress.) Consciousness is subjective and involves qualities, such as the experience of red or the taste of an orange. "Physics aspires to describe the world in entirely objective terms" (Goff 2019, p. 66). Consciousness cannot be understood from this perspective. No matter how well you correlate brain states (readings on an fMRI scan, for instance) with experience, you cannot say what that experience is in its essence.

Goff states that "Materialists who claim *both* that reality can be exhaustively described in the objective vocabulary of physical science *and* that there are subjective [quality-rich] properties are quite simply contradicting themselves" (Goff 2019, p. 68). To address this contradiction, some philosophers, such as Daniel Dennett, have gone so far as to argue that conscious experience is an illusion or a construct of the brain rather than something fundamentally "real." They assert that what we perceive as subjective experience is a complex illusion generated by cognitive processes in the brain. The question this raises is—an illusion to whom? Who is being fooled? Illusionism, as this position is called, is arguably incoherent. Philosopher Galen Strawson has called it "the silliest claim ever made" (Strawson 2018).

Materialistic monism doesn't say that consciousness arises from brain states, but that it is identical with brain states. However, it is simply not within the scope of the physical sciences to support this notion. So back to dualism, but with a twist. Philosopher David Chalmers, famous for coining the phrase "the hard problem" of consciousness, is probably the most well-known proponent of dualistic materialism. His "naturalistic dualism" attempts to reconcile materialism with dualism and is a form of property dualism (as opposed to the substance dualism of Descartes). He sees consciousness as an emergent property of the brain. The brain gives rise to consciousness, but consciousness itself is not material. Naturalistic dualists postulate a separate set of fundamental laws of nature governing this process, similar to the fundamental laws of physics. In this view, consciousness is a fundamental feature of the universe, as is matter.

Most philosophers today reject any form of dualism. One objection is that naturalistic dualism does not eliminate some of the problems inherent in the substance dualism of Descartes. There is still the problem of interaction. Even if the brain, by its complexity, could give rise to conscious experience through upward causation, how would the immaterial mind then influence the brain through downward causation to effect a physical action such as raising an arm or going for a walk?

Another problem with any dualism is that posed by Occam's razor, the principle of parsimony or simplicity. It has been used successfully in philosophy and the sciences since being introduced by William of Ockham in the 14th century. Essentially, it states that, all things being equal, the simplest explanation for a phenomenon, the one with the fewest assumptions, is the best. Do not posit two or three steps to a process when one fits the facts equally. Do not suggest two or three elements to a physical law when one describes the facts equally. The term "razor" refers to the "shaving away" of unnecessary explanations. This principle was instrumental in the development of the Copernican heliocentric model of the universe and Einstein's special theory of relativity. Proponents of monism object to dualism because they feel it adds unnecessary elements to our conception of reality.

That said, Occam's razor is a working principle and not a law. It has been known to sometimes lead scientists down the wrong path. Moreover, the principle of parsimony is not uniformly accepted among scientists and philosophers. Eminent biologist (and materialist) Francis Crick (1916–2004) cautioned against its use in biology. Others have argued that Occam's razor is based on metaphysical assumptions with roots in medieval theological concepts.

As science progresses, more complex explanations do sometimes emerge as the correct ones. As new facts come to light, theories and/or their ramifications often need to increase in complexity. Additional elements must be added to account for new findings, and then more complex explanations become the simplest available that explain the facts as we know them at the time. For example, see the ever-increasing number of subatomic particles postulated to account for the results of physics experiments. This does not negate the usefulness of Occam's razor as a tool in science and philosophy.

Despite materialistic monism's hegemony in modern philosophy, I would contend that most scientists today, and most of the public, are de facto implicit dualists, whether they are materialists or not. I have heard repeatedly among educated peers the concept that consciousness is an epiphenomenon of the brain. Just as medieval Christians thought of themselves as body and soul, we today cannot help but think of ourselves as mind and body as we go about our daily lives.

Where do these dueling theories leave us? Panpsychism to the rescue? Not even thought worthy of consideration by most philosophers a decade ago, it is still a minority position but rising in popularity among academic philosophers and even scientists. Precursors to current theories of panpsychism were proposed by William James (1842–1910), Sir Arthur Eddington (1882–1944), and Bertrand Russell (1872–1970). Panpsychism is the theory that consciousness underlies everything in the universe.

Galen Strawson, one of the most compelling proponents of panpsychism, comes at it from a starting point of physicalism, that everything in the universe is physical. To start, quantum physics tells us there is no "physical stuff" as we conventionally think of it. There are only fields and patterns. The only thing we know for sure is that there is consciousness because we experience it. We assume that there is only one kind of "stuff." (Due to the interaction problem and the principle of parsimony?)

For Strawson, who is an atheist and a physicalist, that physical stuff (statistical fields, energy, patterns) is consciousness "all the way down." He replaces the concept of energy with the concept of experiencing. This is not to say that rocks and socks have experience, but that their subatomic components, whatever those are, do. It is also not saying that particles have memories and emotions. They may have just a rudimentary form of experience, but for Strawson, these aspects of the universe are literally composed of experience.

The traditional materialist view holds that consciousness arises solely in the brains of complex, advanced organisms and has emerged relatively recently in our evolutionary history. As such, it occupies a minuscule fraction of the universe and must emerge countless times—arising separately in each conscious individual. In contrast, panpsychism holds that consciousness is a fundamental and pervasive feature of reality. The purpose of physical science is to tell us only what matter does, not what it is. It tells us nothing about the essential nature of matter "from the inside," or what philosophers call its *intrinsic nature*. For the panpsychist, that intrinsic nature is consciousness.

In a sense, science doesn't *even* tell us what matter does, let alone what it is. For example, in quantum mechanics and field theory, particles are often understood through their roles in equations, rather than through intrinsic properties. Science describes a web of interrelated concepts, in which each property is understood only in terms of its connections to others. Philip Goff describes this circularity, explaining that we cannot know what

> physical properties like "mass" and "charge" are until we know what "force" and "distance" are—because the former are defined in terms of the latter—but until we know what "mass" and "charge" are, we cannot know what "force" and "distance" are—because the latter are defined in terms of the former. (Goff 2019, pp. 176–177)

If science struggles to define matter, it faces even greater challenges in explaining consciousness. In an interview with *Scientific American*, Goff explains that, "Science gives us [only] correlations between brain activity and experience. [...] You can't look inside an electron to see whether or not it is conscious, just as you can't look inside someone's head and see their feelings and experiences" (Cook, 2020). We do know that consciousness exists, so consciousness is a fundamental feature of at least a part of the universe. Panpsychism builds on this to assert that consciousness is a basic constituent of the physical world. Describing Arthur Eddington's panpsychism, Goff states:

> His view was not that particles have two sets of properties: physical properties [...] on the one hand and nonphysical conscious properties on the other. The view is rather that the physical properties of a particle (mass, spin, charge, etc.) *are themselves* forms of consciousness. (Goff 2019, p. 136)

Panpsychism is not without its detractors and vehement criticisms. Panpsychism's own version of the interaction problem is the "combination problem." How do small bits of consciousness combine to form larger, more intricate forms of consciousness? One possible answer would be that evolution took advantage of consciousness as an already present basic constituent of reality. It did not need to create anything out of whole cloth. Because consciousness provided a survival advantage, it evolved into more complex forms.

Other criticisms leveled at panpsychism are that it does not add any explanatory power, that it is not falsifiable, that it doesn't explain everything about the mind-body problem, that there is nothing really that needs explaining, or that consciousness is simply impossible to explain. The "impossible to explain" concept, popularized by philosopher Colin McGinn, is referred to as "mysterianism." The mysterians, as they are sometimes called, generally presuppose materialism and state that the human mind is simply incapable of understanding consciousness. Not only is this far from satisfying; it is based on a priori assumptions about the nature of consciousness and the physical world.

In relation to the "survival hypothesis," the survival of bodily death, I found several variations of panpsychism intriguing. Cosmopsychism says that the universe as a whole is conscious. I find that very appealing, though how someone could ever determine that the entire universe is conscious, I have no idea. Panexperientialism, proposed by David Ray Griffin in the 1970s, says that experience exists throughout the natural world. Griffin described his panexperientialism as a monistic form of physicalism.

What I found most interesting in his book *Unsnarling the World-Knot* (1998) was his discussion of dualism and monism, and in particular "pluralistic monism." Griffin described classical dualism as containing two propositions—that the mind is qualitatively different from the brain and numerically distinct from the brain. In other words, mind and brain are different both in substance and number. He described materialistic monism as also containing two propositions—that there is only one kind of substance, the material, and that the brain and mind are identical. In other words, mind and brain are numerically one thing. Panpsychism, or panexperientialism, is monistic in that the "stuff" of the universe is one thing, and that thing is consciousness. It is pluralistic in that it expresses itself in many things. So the mind and brain can be one thing in substance and two things in quantity. The mind is numerically distinct from the brain. This would solve the interaction problem and should not cause an issue with regard to parsimony, as we see the plurality of nature expressed every day. It is made up of many individual things: rocks, trees, cells, quarks, animals, people, minds, etc.

While strict materialism precludes the possibility of an afterlife, pluralistic monism allows for the survival hypothesis. It also allows for the Eastern concept of a person having multiple energy bodies, which can differ in name and number, depending on the tradition. In Yogic tradition, the five koshas are the physical sheath, the vital energy sheath, the mental body, the wisdom body, and the bliss body. Panpsychism and pluralistic monism make life after death possible, but this does not mean it is a certainty. That question remains open.

The "I" that Binds. A question regarding the possible continuation of consciousness after death is, what exactly might survive? This is not a simple question. This is a question about the nature of self and consciousness and the continuity of the self. At this point in my metaphysical adventures, I am strongly leaning towards the belief that the universe is conscious on some level, or that consciousness is a property of physical reality. The physics, philosophy, parapsychology, and my own experiences have brought me to this conclusion. On this basis, I feel it is likely that, at the very least, our consciousness merges with the "conscious soup" of the universe. In physics, energy is neither lost nor destroyed; it is only transmuted. Since energy, matter, and waves are fundamentally interconnected, and the intrinsic nature of matter may be consciousness, it is more than possible that consciousness is never lost or destroyed—only transmuted. This is cold comfort. And yet, it may be so. Is the "I" that binds us to this slice of space-time continuous through time, or is it discontinuous, merging and re-emerging throughout existence?

What are the other possibilities for continued consciousness after death? One possibility is that you retain awareness and a sense of individual "I" but exist as a free-floating consciousness without a body or location. Another possibility is that you maintain a sense of "I" but with no memories of your past and your family and without your personality, like waking with complete amnesia. You could be present in a different body, environment, or even a different realm or plane of existence. Could this be what reincarnation would feel like? This differs from a quasi-reincarnation that would occur if your consciousness were to merge with Universal Consciousness, and then a part of Universal Consciousness were to separate and reincarnate. In this case, would you still be you?

When exploring what might survive, discussions frequently arise about the unity of the self. Psychologists and philosophers have addressed the unity of consciousness and the unity of the self, though definitions and interpretations vary. Psychologist Phillipe Rochat describes self-unity as "the embodied sense of self as an organized and differentiated entity among other entities" (2019). One philosophical perspective describes a "unified consciousness of self when one is conscious of oneself as the single common subject of experiences of many items in many acts of experiencing" (Brook and Raymont 2021). Then the question arises: Is there an actual unified self?

Philosophers are divided on whether there is a unified self that persists throughout a lifetime, let alone multiple lifetimes or eternity. The debate largely falls into two camps: those who argue for a continuous, unified self and those who challenge this idea. Different spiritual traditions also align with these perspectives. Western traditions generally emphasize a stable, enduring self. Eastern thought offers a more diverse range of views—some support the concept of an unchanging essence, while others reject a fixed self but allow for continuity in a different sense. Overall, Eastern thought tends to view the self as fluid and dynamic, rather than as a fixed, unified entity. Yet even Buddhist thought, which holds the doctrine of *anatta* (or no-self), allows for continuity and rebirth through an ever-changing stream of consciousness.

Personally, I feel fairly certain that the "I" who was a toddler is still the same one I experience today, even though I have no memories from that time, and my personality, intellect, and circumstances are now quite different. The dreaming self, I feel, is the same self who awakens with no memories of some of those dreams. And the self who experiences the dreams remains the same, even if that self looks different and assumes a different identity while dreaming. (I'm sure some philosophers would disagree with my assessment.) Recent research suggests that we maintain conscious experience during all sleep stages—light and deep, REM and non-REM, dreaming and non-dreaming (Windt et al. 2016). However, we don't always lay down memories of these states to be accessible when awake. Similarly, persons with retrograde amnesia were clearly conscious during the period that they can later no longer recall.

Some have looked to unusual cases to further elucidate the existence of a unified self, specifically dissociative identity disorder (formerly called multiple personality disorder) and split-brain phenomena in patients who have had commissurotomies separating the two halves of the brain by cutting the corpus callosum (usually to address intractable epilepsy). While some have argued that in these cases there are literally multiple selves in one body, this is not supported by the evidence. In dissociative identity disorder (DID), there is only one "I" present at a time. Although that identity may be aware of the others, there is no evidence the others have concurrent selves who are independently aware.

Patients who have had commissurotomies function normally most of the time. What's peculiar is that under certain test conditions, each hemisphere appears to be completely unaware of what the other is doing, urging some to claim that there may be two literal centers of consciousness that become unified in normal everyday life. Examples of these phenomena are searchable on the internet. Philosopher Tim Bayne suggests that:

> There are not two centres of consciousness.
> There is just one. What explains the ap-
> pearance of duality is that this single cen-
> tre of consciousness switches in the mate-
> rial of which it is consciousness [sic] from
> one hemisphere to the other. [...] a single
> instance of unified consciousness may be
> switching back and forth between the mate-
> rial in the two hemispheres [with] no duality
> of unified consciousness at any given time.
> (Brook and Raymont 2021)

In thinking about consciousness, self-identity, and what an afterlife might look like, I recalled a brief (momentary, really) experience I have had a number of times. I'd be walking down the street and observing someone on the other side. They could be very different from me in their gender, age, or race. I would start to imagine what it is like to be seeing the world through their eyes, experiencing what they were experiencing—their sights, sounds, and kinesthetic sensations. But my center of consciousness remained with me.

This got me thinking about method acting as a means to further explore the unity of consciousness. I wondered, do the actors ever lose their sense of self and feel as if they are the character? Is there a sense of dual consciousness? Is there only one locus of awareness? How would you even know if there were two loci of awareness when each would only be aware of itself? My husband pointed out that the actor must retain a sense of themself as the actor, or they would simply walk off the stage, no longer in control of their craft.

In *Psychology: An Introduction*, Russell A. Dewey states that "In our culture, multiple personality is approximated by *method acting*. This is the technique by which an actor tries for 'complete emotional identification with a part,' in order to bring that character to life on camera or on the stage" (Dewey 2018). The actors dissociate while remaining psychologically normal.

For clarification, I sat down with Gené Fouché, Senior Lecturer and Department Chair of Theater Arts at McDaniel College in Westminster, MD, and Associate Artistic Director at the Maryland Ensemble Theatre (MET) in Frederick, MD. I asked Professor Fouché about her process as a method actor, what it feels like, and if she ever loses her sense of personal identity and identifies entirely as her character. Fouché described her process as not quite method acting, in that she remains a little more aware of what is going on around her, particularly when backstage. Some actors engage so deeply in the method that you cannot talk to them backstage because they remain completely in character, she explained. Nevertheless, she said that while onstage, you are aware of yourself as the character; you feel and think as the character and lose your sense of yourself.

When pressed to estimate what percentage of herself remains, she said that she is maybe 75 percent the character and 25 percent herself. The 25 percent is just enough to be safe and keep the other actors safe. For instance, in a fight scene, you remember your movements and do not actually hurt each other. That 25 percent is also responsible for figuring out what to do if something goes wrong, such as someone flubbing their lines. The 25 percent is a part of you that is the executive, acting as overall manager (my idea/words, not hers).

Fouché went on to explain that taking on a character begins in the rehearsal process. You build a backstory, internalize your lines so that they become automatic, and embody your motivation and your inner monologue, your inner life. By the time of production, the emotions are real. It doesn't happen often, but there are times during the rehearsal process when, asleep at night, she dreams as the character. There are also times when, during intermission, she realizes she doesn't consciously remember the first act because she has been so "in the zone."

Professor Fouché pointed me in the direction of the 2017 documentary film *Jim & Andy: The Great Beyond*. The film shows what can happen when an actor journeys so deeply into his character that he loses himself. It provides a chronicle of how Jim Carrey adopted the persona of the late comedian Andy Kaufman, as well as Kaufman's alter ego Tony Clifton, over the four-month filming of the 1999 movie *Man on the Moon.* The documentary features interviews with a present-day Jim Carrey and extensive behind-the-scenes footage taken throughout the filming of *Man on the Moon,* during which the actor stayed in character both on and off set.

In a 2017 interview with Josh Rottenberg of the *Los Angeles Times,* Carrey describes his experience of staying in character nearly 24/7 while filming. Though he retained some awareness of himself, Carrey recalls that "pretty much from when [he] woke up to when [he] went to bed, the choices were all [Kaufman's]." As he puts it, "I was just along for the ride." The experience of inhabiting Kaufman for four months proved to be life-changing.

After filming, Carrey struggled to let go of Kaufman and regain his sense of self. In reflecting on the experience, he says, "I was looking back at myself and going, 'What the hell do I believe?'" (Rottenberg 2017). Ultimately, the experience of losing himself profoundly affected Carrey, allowing him to remove the "mask" of the "Jim Carrey" persona and find a deeper reality. For me, this raises the question—how fluid is the self or the personality? Does this offer insight into the concept of reincarnation and shed light on what might survive if it is not what we commonly think of as a personality?

So where does this leave us in the discussion of the "survival hypothesis," as it is called in the parapsychology "survival literature" (not to be confused with survivalist/survival literature for doomsday preppers)? As one would expect, we are left with questions and controversy. Even among parapsychologists who agree on the reality of psi phenomena, there is disagreement about survival.

Six

The Big Five (and a Half)

"To the well-organized mind, death is but the next great adventure."   —Dumbledore to Harry Potter, from *Harry Potter and the Sorcerer's Stone*

J.K. Rowling

These next few chapters discuss topics you **will** find in the New Age section of your local bookstore. There are those who may find this entire discussion ludicrous, especially some hardcore materialists. Nevertheless, there are serious scientists and philosophers who have explored the survival hypothesis. While "survival research" generally presupposes the reality of psychic phenomena, within this group of survival researchers there remain varying levels of skepticism and agnosticism about the reality of an afterlife. They do not take the evidence at face value, and none of them claim certainty.

A considerable number of parapsychologists ultimately conclude that a preponderance of the evidence points to an afterlife, yet several maintain more skepticism, notably philosophers Stephen E. Braude and Michael Sudduth. Sudduth, in particular, denies that the evidence points towards individual or personal survival but does support a more Eastern concept of merging with Universal Consciousness. The skeptical arguments presuppose robust psi and posit that many of the phenomena described ahead in this and the next chapter can be explained by either "living-agent psi" or "super-psi" (that is, manifestations of high levels of psi on the part of living individuals). The controversy can become intense, with publications, rebuttals, rebuttals to rebuttals, and responses to those. Back to "No, it isn't. Yes, it is. No, it isn't. Yes, it is. No, it isn't. Yes, it is." Whatever side of the debate they fall on, and contrary to how they are sometimes portrayed, parapsychologists are highly educated and generally show a substantial degree of intellectual honesty and rigor.

The "big five" that are routinely cited as evidence for postmortem survival are mediumship, near-death experiences (NDEs), reincarnation, apparitions and after-death communications, and end-of-life experiences (including deathbed phenomena such as visions and shared visions). Recently, terminal lucidity (which itself can be considered an end-of-life experience) has been added to the big five. That these phenomena exist is not in question—what they mean is. Of these, only mediumship has been studied in the laboratory, while the others, by their very nature, are largely comprised of anecdotes and case studies. In both NDE and reincarnation research, extensive use has been made of collection, evaluation, categorization, and systematic analysis of case studies. Additionally, there have been both retrospective and prospective studies of NDEs and deathbed phenomena. While most of this research does not rise to the level of laboratory-controlled, double-blinded experimental protocol, the use of case studies is well established in medical and psychological research. As near-death investigator Dr. Bruce Greyson states:

> Most research starts with scientists collecting, verifying, and comparing anecdotes until patterns in these stories become apparent, and then from those patterns emerge hypotheses, which can then be tested and refined. Collections of anecdotes, if they are investigated rigorously, are of immense value in medical research. They were critical, for example, in the discovery of AIDS and Lyme disease, and in discovering unexpected drug effects. (Greyson 2021, p. 61)

Mediumship. The first of the "big five" is mediumship. The history of formal mediumship research dates back to the 19th century, as a subset of psychical research, with the Society for Psychical Research, founded in Britain in 1882, and the American Society for Psychical Research, founded in 1885. Mediumship was brought to widespread popular attention with the Spiritualist movement of the mid-19th century and reached its heyday during and just after World War I, when so many had lost loved ones to the war. Mental mediumship (one form of mediumship) is still being studied today in the laboratory.

Proponents of mediumship research, or research into any of the big five, tend to describe the strongest cases, while skeptics present the weakest cases, often with a mocking and derisive tone. Parapsychologists readily acknowledge that the field and history of mediumship are replete with fraud and credulity. Historically, mediumship investigators have taken great pains to weed out cases of fraud and other possible mundane explanations for the phenomena.

A medium is a psychic who is purportedly able to use their abilities to effect communication between deceased people and the living. It is believed that all mediums have psychic abilities, but not all psychics are mediums. Three forms of mediumship have been researched—physical mediumship, trance mediumship, and mental mediumship.

Physical mediums are those who somehow manifest physical phenomena while acting as go-betweens for the "discarnates." These physical manifestations include "ectoplasm" (melted wax-like shapes resembling hands), tables moving and tilting, and knocking and tapping sounds. These phenomena were extensively investigated in the late 19th and early 20th centuries, and many cases were revealed to be fraudulent. The investigators included scientists and performance magicians, the latter of whom were very familiar with sleight-of-hand techniques. The phenomena occurred almost exclusively in darkened séance rooms, increasing the likelihood of trickery.

Some cases of physical mediumship, especially those involving moving tables and knocking sounds, were judged to be genuine. Even if these occurrences turn out to be genuine, they do little to further the case for the survival hypothesis. They could be examples of living-agent psi. That is, they may be manifestations of the medium's own psychokinesis and not represent actual communication with those who have died.

In his insightful and illuminating book *Immortal Remains: The Evidence for Life After Death,* philosopher and parapsychologist Stephen Braude relates an experience from his days in graduate school when he was a "hard-nosed materialist." He and some friends played a game called "table up," which was an impromptu séance in Braude's own room and in full light. He observed several hours of his own table tipping up and down and heard knocks spelling out coded messages, all the while vigilantly looking for any form of trickery. He states that:

> despite my resistance and lingering skepticism, I was convinced that the observed table movements were genuine. And that conviction hasn't wavered. [...] The table wasn't somebody's prop, and my friends had no opportunity to plant and conceal an apparatus capable of producing the phenomena. [...] I'm certain that only our fingers

touched the top of the table and that they rested lightly on the table's surface. [...] The table rose under our fingers, all fingers were visible atop the table, and I could see clearly that the table made no contact with our legs or knees. In fact, sometimes we rose and stood next to the table, keeping our fingers in contact with the tabletop, and still the table moved up and down under our fingers. I should also add (and I suppose this is important) that we weren't stoned. (Braude 2003, Preface, p. x)

This experience is reminiscent of the "Philip Psychokinesis Experiments," a series of experiments undertaken in 1972 by the Toronto Society for Psychical Research. The group created a fictional ghost character, complete with backstory, much as one would create a character for the theater. They regularly held séances, which resulted in table tilting, levitations, electrical disturbances, and rapping and scratching noises. Philip "communicated" with the group, giving his opinions and filling in additional details of his life. The group concluded that the phenomena were created by their collective manifestation of psychokinesis. Others have suggested that perhaps Philip wasn't entirely fictional and that somehow the group tapped into a real spirit. Regardless, it may be that such physical manifestations are the result of living-agent psi and do not prove the existence of discarnate beings.

Trance mediumship occurs when the medium falls into a trance or altered state of consciousness, and the discarnate appears to speak through them. Both physical and trance mediums were researched heavily by the Society for Psychical Research in the late 19th and first half of the 20th centuries. Much of their work involved exposing charlatans. However, several trance mediums defied all attempts to expose them as frauds, specifically Gladys Leonard and Winifred Coombe Tennant (known as "Mrs. Willet") of London and Leonora Piper of Boston. Mrs. Piper was introduced to the Society by William James, and he considered her to be his "white crow." These particular mediums are cited so often in psychical research that they have become part of the survival research canon. I won't relay further information about them or the investigations around them, as this information is widely available in books and on the internet.

Even if the mediums were completely genuine, it is still possible that, without realizing it, they gained their information through their own highly developed psychic abilities, such as clairvoyance and telepathy—that is, through living-agent psi. Rather than communicating with spirits, they could be "reading the minds" of living individuals or "seeing" objects not present in the room. Proponents of the survival hypothesis cite aspects of trance mediumship phenomena suggestive of contact with actual deceased individuals: (1) That when speaking as the discarnate, the highly vetted mediums often took on the mannerisms and voice qualities of the deceased; (2) The complexity of the information the mediums reported; (3) The fact that the mediums often conveyed information unknown to the sitters (those present to receive messages from or through the medium) at the time of the séance; (4) That the mediums would have had to draw their information from many different sources; and (5) That sometimes the mediums spoke in a language unknown to them.

Those who assert mediumship represents actual communication with the dead state that this level of psychic functioning is not generally observed in other contexts and would have to be a form of "super-psi." The more skeptical or agnostic parapsychologists point out that we do not know the limits of psi in naturalistic settings and that even if the phenomena were genuinely coming from discarnates, it would still presuppose an extraordinary level of psi, both on the part of the medium and the discarnate, to effect communication. Whether it is reasonable or not, the historical and canonical nature of these cases diminishes their evidential impact, at least for me.

Finally, mental mediumship is still being studied today in the laboratory. In mental mediumship, the medium receives messages from the deceased and relays them to the sitter. It is the sort often portrayed on television: "I'm getting a K. Who has someone with a 'K' name who's passed on? They're showing me pink lilies. Does that mean anything to you?" This sort of mediumship is rife with fraud, deception, and delusion, including the use of cold reading techniques, hot reading, and vague information that could apply to anyone. In cold reading, the "psychic" uses high-probability guesses, leading questions, and cues from the sitters to create the appearance of information obtained psychically (sometimes doing so subconsciously or unintentionally). In hot reading, information is deliberately obtained ahead of time through such conceits as audience spies and internet searches. Additional confounding factors can include self-delusion on the part of a medium, and sitter bias, which is the tendency of a sitter to apply whatever the reader says to their own situation.

Current research attempts to control for these and other factors and applies statistical analysis to the data. The Windbridge Research Institute in Tucson, Arizona, is one of several research organizations that have attempted to examine mediumship scientifically. It is the only one I know of still conducting mediumship research, and it is run by Julie Beischel, PhD, and her husband, Mark Boccuzzi. Dr. Beischel received her PhD in pharmacology and toxicology with a minor in microbiology and immunology from the University of Arizona. Her research utilizes strict protocols to eliminate fraud, cold and hot reading, and any subconscious cues. She describes the protocol as:

> "more-than-double-blind" [...] with five levels of blinding: the medium, the sitter, and three researchers are all blinded to different pieces of information. Research readings take place over the phone and only an experimenter (me) and a medium who is in a different city are on the line. The associated sitter knows the reading is happening but does not know which medium is performing it and does not hear the reading as it

takes place. The medium and I have only the first name of a discarnate, which has been emailed to me by a research assistant, and that I give to the medium at the start of the reading. (Beischel 2017, pp. 173–174)

In addition to providing a narrative reading, the medium is asked to respond to a series of questions about the deceased person. To eliminate sitter bias, the medium reads for two different gender-matched discarnates and two sitters. Each sitter then reads both accounts, not knowing which one is meant for them, and is asked to rate which one best matches their deceased loved one. If no psi were operating, one would expect a 50 percent chance that the sitters would choose their own readings. That's not what happens. In describing an experiment involving fifty-eight readings by pre-screened mediums, Dr. Beischel states that "when sitters were [...] instructed [...] to choose one reading or the other in a pair as more applicable to them, even if they weren't entirely confident about their selection, the blinded responses to this 'forced choice' question (as it's called in research) were correct 65.5% of the time" (Beischel 2023, pp. 38–39).

This research does not answer the question of where the correct information or "hits" come from. Do they really come from deceased individuals who continue to exist in another realm, or from general psychic information obtained through living-agent psi? The Windbridge Institute attempts to address this question with further research. Mediums themselves (who are also psychics) say that they often can feel a significant difference between information received psychically and communication coming directly from discarnates.

To test this assertion, Windbridge designed an experiment in which ten pre-screened mediums were given two first names to read for (with no other information provided). The target individuals were matched for age and gender. However, some of the targets were deceased, while others were still living. The mediums were then asked to ascertain which information was coming from a deceased individual, from a living individual, or if both were living or deceased. The mediums guessed correctly with 74 percent accuracy, when 50 percent would have been expected by chance (Beischel 2023, p. 66). This may still be the result of living-agent psi. Intriguingly, when the phenomenology of the mediums' experience during readings was examined, one clear difference was reported between readings for deceased and living individuals, and that was a feeling or impression of love. (Yes, I know how corny and sappy this sounds.) Mediums had reported this previously in a questionnaire, and it was reported again about the readings for this study. The mediums reported stronger feelings and impressions of love when reading for deceased rather than living targets, and this tended to hold even when they incorrectly identified whether the target was living or deceased.

Dean Radin and his team performed a similar experiment involving twelve mediums and 404 photos, half of deceased and half of living persons. The results were statistically significant, but not overwhelming, with an overall hit rate of 53.8 percent, where 50 percent would be expected by chance. The mediums' electrical brain activity was monitored during the task, and a "robust effect" was observed while the mediums

> were looking at the photos. At 100 milliseconds after the photo was displayed on the monitor, which is before the mediums could consciously decide how they were going to respond, their brains showed different patterns of activity when they correctly decided if the person was alive or dead, as compared to when their decision was incorrect. (Radin 2018, p. 162)

There were additional unanticipated findings suggestive of the possibility of reincarnation:

> The mediums' performance was much more accurate with the "newly deceased" (56.8 percent correct) than with the "older deceased" (51.7 percent) or the "long deceased" (50.2 percent). This result, which surprised us, suggests a possible way to experimentally explore the idea of reincarnation, because mediums sometimes report that a person who passed away long ago no longer "feels" dead, presumably because that person (or some aspect of that person's spirit) has gone on to another incarnation. (Radin 2018, p. 161)

As mentioned, even if mediumship genuinely provides accurate information, this does not prove continuing existence beyond death, as the information could be accessed through living-agent psi. Despite this, I decided to find out for myself what it would be like to have a mediumship reading. I've described previously here my experience with the mediumship circle where I received a startling possible communication from my mother-in-law. Lee was not in any way on my conscious mind, and in fact, at first, I had no idea who the medium was talking about. She certainly didn't obtain the information psychically from my conscious mind. Is it possible she obtained it from my subconscious or other psychically available "cosmic soup?"

I have since had an additional mediumship reading from a Windbridge-certified medium. The reading was spectacularly off. The medium asked non-stop leading questions such as, "I'm getting the name George. Does that mean anything to you? I'm getting it has to do with the state of Georgia. Does that mean anything to you?" And then, "Well, what was your grandfather's name? What was your mother's name? I see root vegetables. I see orange food. Was she a good cook? (She was okay.) Did she wear sweaters? (Don't most women wear sweaters?) Did she knit? (No.) Was she cold a lot at the end of her life? Did she have breathing problems?" Aren't most elderly people cold? Don't most people have breathing problems at the end of their lives? One would have to work hard to get as many misses as she did in a 45-minute period. Only one word made any sense, "violin." Then she went on to say a bass violin or cello. (Nope.) After a while, with my continual responses of "No," she said it wasn't working for her and that that can occasionally happen, although rarely.

As I look over the above description of my mediumship reading during proofreading, I realize there were several "hits" that I didn't notice at the time. I really did enjoy my mother's sweet potato dish (orange root vegetable). My grandfather did play the violin professionally, although not the bass violin or cello. He was stationed in Georgia for boot camp during World War I, and my brother has a photo of his entire regiment on his wall. And my father referred to a "George" while on his deathbed (more about this later). Were these an example of the medium throwing out words and seeing what sticks? Is my notice of them an example of sitter bias?

Near-Death Experiences. The second of the "big five" is near-death experiences (NDEs). In 1975, Dr. Raymond Moody's book *Life After Life* brought the term near-death experience into the popular vernacular. Since that time, quite a few near-death researchers have been collecting case studies and surveys from experiencers and developing retrospective and prospective studies. Notable among near-death investigators are psychiatrist Dr. Bruce Greyson (professor of psychiatry and neurobehavioral sciences at the University of Virginia Medical School), radiation oncologist Dr. Jeffrey Long, cardiologist Dr. Pim van Lommel, neuropsychiatrist Dr. Peter Fenwick, and Dr. Sam Parnia (pulmonologist and critical care physician).

Systematic prospective studies of survivors of cardiac arrest have been conducted by Van Lommel, Greyson, Parnia, and others, including Van Lommel's 2001 study published in *The Lancet*. They describe a core set of experiences reported by near-death survivors, many ostensibly occurring during unconsciousness when the person is close to death. Often their hearts have stopped, and they have no brainwave activity visible on an EEG. While much of the research is anecdotal, many thousands of NDE reports have been compiled, analyzed, and categorized, and research also involves questionnaires and surveys. The phenomenology of near-death experiences includes the following:

1. A sense of leaving the body (OBE, as described in Chapter Three), seeing the body from above, observing resuscitation attempts, and perceiving activities in the nearby vicinity.

2. Traveling through a tunnel to a different realm.

3. Encountering a brilliant light or a being of light.

4. Experiencing a complete life review.

5. Meeting deceased relatives or other beings.

6. A sense of peace and love.

7. Reaching a border and being told or deciding to go back.

8. Increased clarity and vividness of perceptions with increased clarity and lucidity of thought and a distorted sense of time.

9. Ineffability—the impossibility of adequately expressing the experience in words.

Approximately 10 to 20 percent of people who come close to death report a near-death experience, and most of those who report these experiences have no doubt as to their reality. They describe them as not at all dreamlike and "realer than real." However, most do not experience all of the above features of an NDE, and some report only a few, raising the question of whether there is an actual core experience. There is also the question of whether these experiences occur during the time of unconsciousness or as the person is coming back into consciousness.

Near-death investigators highlight some interesting characteristics of NDEs and the people who have had an NDE. Investigations compared patients who have come close to death without experiencing an NDE with those who have experienced an NDE. Both groups are equivalent in terms of religious, social, and educational backgrounds, and include atheists and agnostics. However, those who have had NDEs report increased compassion, a new sense of purpose, less concern about status and material accumulation, increased self-esteem, increased joy, and significantly decreased fear of death. These changes have also been corroborated by friends and family of the NDE experiencers. This is in stark contrast to those who came close to death but did not have an NDE. They often experience increased fear of death and PTSD-like symptoms.

Other compelling findings from near-death research involve aspects of NDE memories. Studies that examine memories of near-death experiences find that, in contrast to memories of dreams and hallucinations, NDE memories do not fade or change with time. They are recalled vividly and without alteration, even years after the experience. Moreover, when NDEers (as they are often called) report meeting others during their NDE, the others are almost always deceased people, not living people as one would expect in a hallucination.

NDE skeptics argue that the NDE is a hallucination of the dying brain. They claim that the features of an NDE can be explained by temporal lobe seizures, a lack of oxygen to the brain, metabolic disturbances, the effect of medications, and other similar factors. NDE researchers have convincingly refuted these explanations, pointing out that there are significant differences in the phenomenology of NDEs and these other cases. Still, concerning NDEs and their relationship to consciousness after death, questions remain. One, as noted earlier, is when exactly did the experience occur? Did it occur when the experiencer was unconscious and possibly without heartbeat and brainwave activity, or did it happen as they were coming back into consciousness?

The only phenomenon that could clarify when the NDE actually occurs is the out-of-body experience. Approximately half of NDE experiencers describe seeing activities from a perspective outside the body. The reports of interest are those of veridical experiences—those later verified by independent witnesses—especially experiences that occurred during known times of unconsciousness. And there are hundreds of such reports. They are recounted in almost every book and article on NDEs.

Dr. Bruce Greyson tells of an incident that happened early in his career as a psychiatrist. While eating in the hospital cafeteria, his pager suddenly went off, startling him and causing him to splatter spaghetti sauce on his tie. Quickly, he hid the stain under his lab coat. He was being called to the emergency room to see a young woman, Holly, who had overdosed in a suicide attempt and was still unconscious. In the family lounge down the hall, Greyson spoke with Holly's roommate. Forgetting about the splattered sauce, he unbuttoned his lab coat, revealing the stained tie. The next morning, after Holly had awakened, Greyson introduced himself to her. To his surprise, she said, "I know who you are. I remember you from last night. [...] I saw you talking with Susan, sitting on the couch. [...] You were wearing a striped tie that had a red stain on it." She then repeated the conversation Greyson had had with Susan. Greyson didn't know how to process the experience and pushed it to the back of his mind, continuing his traditional and successful career as an academic psychiatrist. Several years later, he met Dr. Raymond Moody and learned that Holly's experience was not unique. "That revelation grabbed [his] attention, and launched [him] on a journey to follow an evidence-based approach to NDEs" (Greyson 2021, pp. 1–6).

Some of the more spectacular reports of veridical NDEs have been repeated so many times that they have reached the status of legend. For me, their legendary status has the effect of diminishing their evidential impact. One of the most widely cited NDE cases is "The Shoe on the Ledge." You can find it in a Google search, with descriptions by both its proponents and critics, and with credible rebuttals to its criticism. Many NDE reports are extremely compelling, and anyone who has experienced this phenomenon directly, as either the NDE experiencer or the person verifying the experience, could be quite convinced. For obvious reasons, this is not a personal white crow I will be seeking.

Two small studies support the significance of the NDE as an indicator of consciousness beyond the brain and strongly suggest that NDEs occur during known periods of unconsciousness. These studies were published by Michael Sabom, MD, in 1982 and Penny Sartori, PhD, in 2004. In both studies, patients who had experienced cardiac arrest were divided into two groups: those who reported an NDE that included out-of-body experiences with visual perception of the local vicinity and those who did not report any NDE. They were asked to describe their own resuscitation process. Those who had had NDEs were highly accurate in their descriptions, while those who had not were highly inaccurate.

Recent research has discovered that in deep coma and at the time of death, even when the EEG has flatlined, there is a surge of brain activity at the deeper TPJ region of the brain, the junction between the temporal, parietal, and occipital lobes (Gray 2023). The TPJ region is associated with dreaming, hallucinations, and altered states. Other studies have found a surge of gamma waves in rats at the time of death, and a similar pattern was found in two of four comatose patients when they were removed from life support (Sullivan 2023). Gamma waves are associated with consciousness, attention, and memory.

In an interview with Megan Brooks for *Medical News*, Sam Parnia describes a study "that examined consciousness and its underlying electrocortical biomarkers during CPR." Fewer than 10 percent of the patients survived, and a little more than half of those completed interviews. Of those, only eleven individuals, approximately 10 percent, reported lucid NDE experiences. They found that near-normal physiologic EEG activity resumed 35 to 60 minutes into CPR, and that the NDE experiencers described separation from their bodies, "observing events without pain or distress," and a meaningful retrospective evaluation of their lives (Brooks 2022).

What does this mean in terms of the brain's role in consciousness and the NDE? One could speculate that the NDE, and by analogy consciousness, is caused by a functioning brain. On the other hand, the usual brain mechanisms involved in consciousness appear to be severely compromised, which would ordinarily cause significantly reduced or impaired consciousness. In addition, if the brain is a consciousness filter, would there have to be some sort of brain function present to interface with the physical person and to lay down the memories to be accessed later?

These findings do not explain the fact that NDEs are lucid, usually involve visions of deceased rather than living people, and sometimes involve veridical perceptions from perspectives outside the body while unconscious. About the NDE, Dean Radin states, "Given that near-death is a prime example of a non-ordinary state of consciousness, it may be that some of the strikingly vivid aspects of NDEs arise because clearer forms of psi perception are suppressed by a normally functioning brain" (Radin 2018, p. 158). So the NDE could be an example of vivid living-agent psi consistent with quantum mechanics and a panpsychist view of reality, rather than an actual separation of consciousness from the body. (This is also true for the OBE, described in Chapter Three, which occurs in an altered state.) In any case, it would make sense that there would be a part of the brain still active during NDEs to interface with the physical organism and bring memories back into conscious awareness in ordinary reality. This, however, would raise the question of how memories are brought into the physical with reincarnation, a subject in the next chapter.

Finally, most NDE research relies primarily on analyzing case studies and subjective reports of private experiences that cannot be directly observed. We know that people do misremember, confabulate, embellish, and tell tales, and they can be poor judges of their own lucidity when in an altered state. Given the more than eight billion people on earth, it is easy to see how thousands of these could report convincing NDEs. Additionally, every person who has reported an NDE ultimately survived, so perhaps even if consciousness is not in the brain, its manifestation may rely on being associated with a living person.

Seven

The Big Five (and a Half) Continued

All journeys have secret destinations of which the traveler is unaware.   —from *The Legend of the Baal-Shem*

Martin Buber

Reincarnation. Several survival researchers believe that reincarnation studies offer the strongest evidence for the survival hypothesis. Psychiatrist Dr. Ian Stevenson (1918–2007), former head of the psychiatry department at the University of Virginia, began his investigations of children's past-life memories in 1961. He collected thousands of case studies, focusing most of his work in India and other regions where belief in reincarnation is prevalent. His later studies did include cases from the West, including the United States, the UK, and Europe. Psychiatrist Dr. Jim Tucker, Director of the Division of Perceptual

Studies at the University of Virginia Health System, has continued Dr. Stevenson's work and continues to investigate "cases of the reincarnation type" (as they are called in the literature), primarily in the West, where reincarnation is not the prevailing belief.

Reincarnation research is more than just "story collection." Serious researchers investigate the child's claims and attempt to identify a previous personality (PP). The child's statements regarding the identified previous personality are examined for accuracy. Upon investigation, the children are shown to have knowledge of details and events from the PP that they could not have gained in any ordinary manner. The stronger cases are those investigated before the parents identify any previous personality and, ideally, early on when the memories begin to surface. Researchers also attempt to reduce or eliminate alternative explanations such as fraud, imagination, conscious or unconscious parental motivations, memory distortions on the part of witnesses, or other sources of information for a child's purported past life memories, such as public information, family photos, and overheard conversations.

These cases often start with a child's statement to a parent, such as, "I miss my other family. I want to see my other mommy," or "When I was your grandma, I used to dress you like this." The children usually spontaneously begin speaking about a past life sometime between two and four years of age and generally lose those past-life memories around the age of six or seven. They express their past-life memories in the first person, in many cases with strong emotion. Some children reenact their mode of death in a previous life or have significant phobias regarding how they died, such as a fear of water due to drowning. Some even report memories from between lives.

Reincarnation research, by its very nature, relies on investigation and analysis of case studies and does not lend itself to prospective laboratory examination. The strongest cases have become part of the survival legends, complete with debunking and rebuttals to the debunking. If you Google search "James Leininger reincarnation," you will find the descriptions of, and criticisms of, the James Leininger reincarnation case, and rebuttals to the criticism. For an analysis of various criticisms of reincarnation research, assessing the strengths and weaknesses of both the research and its critiques, refer to psi-encyclopedia.spr.ac.uk/articles/criticisms-reinca rnation-case-studies. Here is some of the back-and-forth:

1. "The Case of James Leininger: An American Case of the Reincarnation Type." https://pubmed.ncb i.nlm.nih.gov/27079216/ (Tucker 2016).

2. "The James Leininger Case Re-Examined." *Journal of Scientific Exploration.* https://journalofscientificexploration. org/index.php/jse/article/view/2361 (Sudduth 2021).

3. "Response to Sudduth's 'James Leininger Case Re-Examined.'" *Journal of Scientific Exploration.* https://www.researchgate.net/publication/360

821061_Response_to_Sudduth's_James_Leining er_Case_Re-Examine (Tucker 2022).

Parapsychologists who are either antagonistic to or agnostic about cases of the reincarnation type (CORT) cite the possibility of living-agent psi as a source for the child's memories. Is the child possibly tapping into the consciousness of a deceased person who is still accessible through the collective unconscious? The children themselves do not experience it that way. They express the memories as their own. Furthermore, in general, the children do not show any other psychic abilities whatsoever. So why would they in this one situation? Psychological testing reveals the children to be psychologically healthy and not prone to fantasy.

Further support suggestive of reincarnation is seen in statistical analysis of the cases. Consistently across cultures, a high percentage of children with past-life memories report having died an unnatural death. As Jim Tucker describes, these children

> recall a largely nondescript life of a person who typically lived fairly close by [...]. The one part of the life that is often out of the ordinary is how the previous person died. Around 70 percent of the children describe a life that ended in an unnatural death, such as murder, suicide, accident, or combat. (Tucker 2017, p. 47)

Why would they describe very ordinary lives, but with non-ordinary modes of death, consistently across cultures? Would someone who died a violent death be more likely to carry memories into the next life? Or are these simply the types of deaths children are exposed to in stories and on television?

Apparitions and After-Death Communication. What the public popularly refers to as "ghosts" is described as three very different phenomena by parapsychologists and paranormal investigators. Hauntings and poltergeists are not suggestive of survival, while apparitions may be. All these phenomena have been reported throughout the centuries and investigated and well documented in the last several hundred years. Most common are hauntings, which parapsychologist Loyd Auerbach characterizes as sightings of figures, unexplained sounds and voices, smells, and other sensations that individuals attribute to the presence of a ghost. These "ghosts seem to be acting in repetitive patterns and are essentially locked to a location such as a house, bar, restaurant, hotel, plot of land, or on rarer occasion to an object" (Auerbach 2017, p. 250). They do not appear to be conscious or to interact with the living in any way. Auerbach further explains that:

> A haunting is a kind of echo, or recording of sorts, of actual people and events. A location (or object) holds/records information about

its history. Our own psychic abilities—or perhaps our brains, interacting with some element of the physical environment—allow us to pick up certain playbacks of this history. (Auerbach 2017, p. 250)

Poltergeists, on the other hand, are believed to be caused by psychokinesis on the part of a living person, often a troubled adolescent in the home. These PK manifestations can result in noises, electrical malfunctions, and objects moving and breaking, seemingly on their own.

Of interest to the case for survival are interactive apparitions that appear to be aware of their environment and that interact with the living. There are thousands of thoroughly investigated, credible, and well-documented cases, some with multiple witnesses simultaneously or separately perceiving and interacting with the same apparition. These perceptions are usually visual, often auditory, and sometimes tactile, and a large percentage occur during the day when the percipient is fully awake.

Systematic investigations of such apparitions began with the Society for Psychical Research and the American Society for Psychical Research in the 1800s. More recently, Erlendur Haraldsson (1931–2020), Loyd Auerbach, and other parapsychologists have continued these investigations. They consider alternative, non-paranormal explanations for apparitions, such as faulty memory, exaggeration, collusion, hypnogogic and hypnopompic images (images while falling asleep and waking up, respectively), suggestion, and expectation. While there are numerous credible investigations into apparitions, they rely predominantly on suggestive anecdotal evidence. To those who have experienced these apparitions, they are highly evidential on a personal level, but they do not constitute scientific proof.

In a subset of apparitions that also fall under the category of after-death communication, the deceased appears to a friend or family member around the time of death. This frequently occurs before the percipient knows that their loved one has died or even that they were ill and often coincides with the moment of death. Some of these apparitions appear to multiple witnesses, in the same room or separated by vast distances, simultaneously or in close succession. Some encounters happen years after the death yet provide veridical information not previously known to the percipient.

Quite a few striking examples of these sorts of apparitions are described in the literature, several of which are presented in Leslie Kean's fascinating book *Surviving Death* (2017). Living-agent psi cannot be categorically ruled out, nor can other mundane explanations, and again, the evidence is primarily anecdotal. It would seem that living-agent psi would be unlikely when there were multiple witnesses, and most of those were not known to be particularly psychic. As Auerbach lucidly points out:

> If there is no upper limit to psi's range or strength, which itself is as non-falsifiable as the survival hypothesis, this can always be used to explain any paranormal experience,

> no matter how unusual or complex. After all,
> an interactive dead person may be just as
> difficult to conceptualize as unlimited psi by
> those who have not experienced something
> like this themselves. (Auerbach 2017, p. 265)

As mentioned, apparitions can be a form of after-death communication (ADC). But there are other forms of ADC. The more subtle ADCs come in the form of smells, feelings of a presence, electrical disturbances, tactile sensations, auditory impressions, symbolic objects, orbs of light, and ADCs experienced in dreams. Others are more dramatic, such as moving objects, loud voices relaying messages, and incomplete messages received by more than one person that, when combined, form a complete and meaningful communication. A remarkable account of this sort of composite communication is detailed in Chapter 19 of Kean's book.

Research into after-death communication began in the mid-19th century and continues today. It is comprised largely of collections and analyses of anecdotal material. The phenomena included in the various studies can differ. Some studies include encounters during dreams, while others do not. Some include apparitions appearing at the time of death, while others do not. There appears to be agreement on several aspects of after-death communication, even in the more mainstream medical literature—that ADC happens and is not uncommon, that it can be a normal part of grieving and is in no way a sign of psychopathology, and that it brings comfort to the grieving. In addition, those who have experienced ADCs report increased spirituality, though not religiosity, and decreased fear of death.

Leslie Kean defines after-death communications as "spontaneous, personal signals perceived as coming from a departed loved one, which seem unmistakably clear and highly meaningful to the one receiving them" (Kean 2017, p. 224). Some of these are more easily explained by ordinary processes, while others seem highly evidential. Examples of more ordinary explanations for lights flickering or turning on and off could include overloaded circuits, voltage fluctuations, utility service issues, and fluctuating demand. A cap exploding from a cooking oil bottle (an incident cited by Kean) could be caused by oil that has particulate food matter beginning to ferment or other spoilage causing a buildup of gas. Visual apparitions and auditory impressions that appear to be coming from the environment could be related to hypnagogic and hypnopompic phenomena that occur at the borders of sleep. I have had such an experience.

In the 1990s, we had a special pet rabbit named Jumpy. About a week after she died, I was convinced that I heard her thumping while I was fully awake lying in bed. Over the next several years, I began to hear loud bangs while either falling asleep or waking in the middle of the night, although sometimes I felt as if I were alert and fully awake. They sounded as if they were very real, outside my mind, and coming from within the house. Each time, I would get up and investigate, convinced that something large had fallen, a door had slammed, or someone was trying to break in. Inevitably, all was quiet, and nothing had been disturbed.

It turns out that I had developed "exploding head syndrome," a benign sleep condition that causes the sensation of hearing a loud sound during sleep-wake/wake-sleep transitions. This sometimes still happens, and when it does, I say to myself, "Oh, there it is again," and go back to sleep. Similarly, in sleep paralysis, which also occurs during the transitions, you feel as if you are awake but unable to move your body. Some people may see figures or have unusual or frightening sensations.

There are, however, some striking and compelling examples of after-death communications that are harder to explain. Several highly suggestive ones are described in Chapter 19 of Leslie Kean's book. And a particularly convincing after-death communication is reported in *Scientific American* by none other than uber-skeptic and professional debunker of all things paranormal, Michael Shermer. Shermer is the executive director of The Skeptics Society and founding publisher of *Skeptic* magazine, a publication focused on investigating pseudoscientific and supernatural claims. He is a person who would not be inclined towards delusion or fabrication.

In the October 2014 issue of *Scientific American,* Shermer describes an event that he says was "so mysterious that it shook [his] skepticism." On the day of his wedding, his fiancée, Jennifer Graf, expressed sadness that her grandfather, who had been a father figure to her, could not be there to give her away. He had died many years earlier and had left her a 1978 Philips transistor radio, which was precious to her and which no longer worked. Several months before the wedding, Shermer had tried to get it working. He finally gave up and put it out of sight in a drawer. On the day of the wedding, which was held in their home, they suddenly heard music playing. It was the radio playing a love song. Shermer's daughter said she had heard the music just as the ceremony was beginning. "My grandfather is here with us. I'm not alone," said Graf. The radio continued to play the rest of that day, then stopped, and it has not worked since.

In the article, Shermer goes on to say that if this had happened to someone else, he would explain it as a "chance electrical anomaly" combined with coincidence and the "law of large numbers." However, the emotional impact at the time was such that he states, "It rocked me back on my heels and shook my skepticism to its core." He urges his readers to "take seriously the scientific credo to keep an open mind and remain agnostic when the evidence is indecisive or the riddle unsolved" (Shermer 2014). This sentiment was short-lived, and the shaking of skepticism was brief with limited impact. Shermer continues to remain an outspoken skeptic and denier of even the *possibility* of anything paranormal. While the stories of after-death communication do not serve as scientific proof of an afterlife, they can be quite evidential to those who experience them (although not to Shermer).

End-of-Life Experiences. With the advent of hospice care in the late 1960s, palliative care in the late 1980s, and an increasing concern for end-of-life care in general, there has been a surge in research regarding end-of-life experiences. (It wasn't until 2006 that the American Board of Medical Specialties [ABMS] recognized hospice and palliative care as a specialty.) By 2019, when my mother was in hospice, family members commonly received literature describing what they might expect in the last days. This included end-of-life experiences (ELEs) such as the patient's visions and visits from departed loved ones and other spirits, and terminal lucidity, or a surge in energy and clarity not long before dying.

Indeed, I did see my mother look up from sleep and say to someone unseen by me, "Oh, what are you doing here?" And in 1991, the day before my father died, my mother, brother, and I observed him gazing into a far corner of the room. "Look at George. He is so beautiful," my father exclaimed. "George? George who? George Bush?" we asked. "Don't insult my George that way!" responded my father. We did not know what to make of that, but at the time we assumed it was caused by a confusional state of the dying brain. Here are two links to hospice literature provided to families and caregivers:

- www.crossroadshospice.com/hospice-palliative-care-blog/2017/july/19/understanding-end-of-life-visions/

- www.crossroadshospice.com/hospice-palliative-care-blog/2019/july/16/end-of-life-rallying-what-is-terminal-lucidity/.

The first serious examination of deathbed visions and visits was conducted by physics professor Sir William Barrett (1844–1925) of the Royal College of Science in Dublin in the 1920s. His interest was aroused when his wife, an obstetrician, described a case she had witnessed personally. One of her patients, as she lay dying, reported seeing deceased family members, including her sister, who, unbeknown to the patient, had died three weeks earlier. Barrett retells this episode in his book *Death-Bed Visions* (1926), in a chapter entitled "Visions Seen by the Dying of Persons by Them Unknown to be Dead."

From 1959 to 1973, Erlendur Haraldsson and Karlis Osis (1917–1997) conducted studies of deathbed phenomena based on large amounts of data collected through surveys and interviews of physicians and nurses in both India and the United States. The data were then "subjected to elaborate statistical, pattern, and content analysis through computer evaluation" (Haraldsson and Osis 2012, p. 2). They wanted "to know to what extent these experiences are affected by certain medical, psychiatric, psychological, and cultural factors, including religious upbringing" (p. xvi).

A more recent study published in 2010, "Comfort for the Dying: Five Year Retrospective and One Year Prospective Studies of End-of-Life Experiences," published in the *Archives of Gerontology and Geriatrics,* was conducted by Peter Fenwick, Sue Brayne, and Hilary Lovelace (Fenwick et al. 2010). One of their notable findings is that higher levels of mental clarity tend to increase, rather than decrease, the patients' experience of visions. Or perhaps it is that patients are better able to relay their visions to family members when they experience increased clarity.

While simultaneously seeing visions of deceased loved ones, patients are often fully oriented, aware of their surroundings, and able to communicate lucidly with others in the room. The hallucinations do not appear to be drug-induced, as drug-induced hallucinations are different in quality and often confusional. Also, the apparitions are almost always reported as having a take-away message, such as, "I will be back for you soon," and patients appear to be comforted. This is in contrast to visions described in near-death experiences, which almost always relay messages such as, "Go back. It is not your time."

Some intriguing cases involve reports by family and medical caregivers who participate in the deathbed visions. Numerous firsthand accounts (sometimes from multiple witnesses at the bedside) describe unexplained lights in the room, figures of light, or shapes and mists leaving the body at the moment of death. Shared death experiences (SDEs) are phenomena experienced not only by the dying but also by healthy individuals present at the bedside. These may include apparitions of deceased relatives, unexplained voices and music, and visions of other realms. While the consensus of investigations into these cases is that they cannot be attributed to hypoxia, medications, delirium, or other medical issues common at the end of life, ultimately, these studies are based on anecdotal evidence that is then systematically analyzed.

All of these reports of end-of-life phenomena are suggestive of an afterlife but do not provide conclusive proof.

Again, this is not a personal white crow I would seek out, but the next best thing was reading Hadley Vlahos' poignant and captivating book *The In-Between: Unforgettable Encounters During Life's Final Moments*. In this memoir of her experiences as a hospice nurse, Vlahos shares stories of patients' final days, including accounts of their end-of-life visits from deceased relatives. These are not told from the view of a philosopher or a scientist, but from a deeply personal perspective.

In her conclusion, Vlahos writes that end-of-life visitations occur equally for believers and non-believers alike. She reflects, "I do believe that our loved ones come to get us when we pass, and I don't believe that's the result of a chemical reaction in our brain in those final hours," observing that unlike hallucinations—in which patients see distorted or nonsensical imagery—these encounters are lucid and meaningful to those experiencing them (Vlahos 2023, pp. 249–250).

Such accounts of end-of-life visitations, which can be quite compelling, offer insight into consciousness and the dying process, making them a valuable area of study. Investigating end-of-life experiences offers a unique advantage over studying near-death experiences. While anecdotal, these accounts often involve outside witnesses observing events in real time. This is especially true for cases of terminal lucidity, the subject of the next section.

Terminal Lucidity. Just recently come to the attention of researchers is terminal lucidity (TL), or paradoxical lucidity (PL), and yet it has already become a well-established phenomenon. It is described as a return to mental clarity in someone who had previously lost memory function, coherent thought, and the ability to communicate due to severe neurological and psychiatric disorders such as late-stage Alzheimer's and other dementias, severe chronic schizophrenia, brain tumors, and stroke.

This lucid episode often occurs just minutes to hours before death, sometimes days, and rarely a week or two. The episodes can be as short as several minutes or may last hours or a day. Typically, the patient shows a sudden return of memories and personality, orientation, cognition, and coherent speech. They recognize their family members and engage in meaningful conversation—requesting food, asking family members about their lives, getting their affairs in order, and saying goodbyes. This "end-of-life rallying" (as it is described in some hospice literature) can be confusing to family members who may think their loved one is getting better, only to see them die in the next hours or days.

Anecdotal case reports of lucid episodes are evident in the medical literature of the 18th and 19th centuries; however, the phenomenon was largely ignored during the 20th century. It came to the attention of researchers when biologist Michael Nahm coined the phrase "terminal lucidity" in 2009. He provided a historical overview dating back to Hippocrates, with emphasis on anecdotal cases from the 19th century (Nahm 2010). Currently, research is in its infancy but ongoing. Terminal lucidity has been referred to as both common and uncommon in the literature. Some reports put the prevalence at around 10 percent in dementia patients near death, with 84 percent of those with terminal lucidity dying within a week.

Predictably, researchers approach TL from different a priori assumptions. George A. Mashour et al., in their article for *Alzheimer's & Dementia* (2019), state right up front that they "review relevant research on the phenomenon of PL as well as its biological plausibility, draw connections across the evidence base to begin to formulate a *mechanistic model*" (emphasis mine). Mashour goes on to propose that "the dying or hypoxic brain can generate neurochemical and neuroelectrical surges that might be associated with the network dynamics of complex systems and that might generate spontaneous network integration manifesting as lucid behavior," and that:

> Because the episodes of PL occur rather suddenly, it is unlikely that regeneration of neurons can account for them. Such fluctuations may reflect complex adjustments in signaling cascades, synaptic modifications, neuronal network interactions, and, perhaps, temporary reversal of, or compensation for, chronic functional inhibition due to neurotoxic proteins. (Mashour 2019)

I'm not sure I fully understand that, but it seems safe to say that his mechanistic view presupposes materialism. Additionally, it is replete with "might," "may," and "perhaps," and indefinite concepts such as "network dynamics" and "network integration." While there may eventually be an explanation for TL based on brain physiology, Mashour's proposition is highly speculative and assumes a mechanistic paradigm. Even if a physiological basis for TL were ultimately found, it would still rely on correlation rather than causation.

Researchers in favor of the survival hypothesis propose that the phenomenon of terminal lucidity supports the concept that consciousness is not produced by the brain. For instance, Alzheimer's disease, the most common form of dementia, is progressive and irreversible. It results in extreme shrinkage of the cerebral cortex and hippocampus, atypical clumps and tangles of proteins between and within neurons, and significant neuronal degradation and areas of brain death. About terminal lucidity, psychologist Dr. Marilyn A. Mendoza notes that "normal cognition can occur in spite of a severely damaged brain" and asks, "How is it possible for someone's brain to be destroyed by a disease, and yet the person can become lucid and engaging close to death?" (Mendoza 2018).

Supporters of the survival hypothesis assert that the TL evidence does not stand alone. When considering the evidence as a whole—terminal lucidity, mediumship studies, near-death experiences, end-of-life visions, apparitions and after-death communications, and cases of the reincarnation type—they claim the evidence is overwhelming. Could each of these areas of research be flawed? If so, would their combined evidence also be flawed, or would their independent findings still align to suggest a real phenomenon? Is the evidence flawed, or does it point to something real?

Proponents of survival often draw an analogy between evidential standards used in legal cases and those applied to survival research, citing concepts such as "a preponderance of the evidence" and "beyond a reasonable doubt." Sociologist Leo Ruickbie states, "A common standard for deciding cases where the stakes are high [...] is found in the legal system: it must be 'beyond reasonable doubt.'" However, like the concept of "extraordinary evidence," the term "reasonable doubt" lacks a concrete, independent definition, making its application difficult. Ruickbie quotes the Federal Judicial Center's instructions to jurors as follows: "Proof beyond a reasonable doubt is proof that leaves you firmly convinced [...]. There are very few things in this world that we know with absolute certainty, and [...] the law does not require proof that overcomes every possible doubt." He adds that "firmly convinced" could be considered just as circular as "beyond a reasonable doubt" (in that it defines one vague concept with another), but emphasizes that proof does not need to answer "every possible doubt" (Ruickbie 2023, pp. 9–10).

Of course, the legal system is imperfect—sometimes the innocent are convicted, and the guilty go free. Yet much like democracy, while imperfect, it is the best system available. Ultimately, the arguments depend on the assumptions you start with and what you are willing to accept as evidence. Emotions run high, and preconceptions are entrenched on both sides of the afterlife question. For the individual, a personal white crow experience could tip the balance.

Eight

Towards Enchantment

There are more things in Heaven and Earth,
Horatio, than are dreamt of in your philosophy.
—from *Hamlet*

William Shakespeare

Sociologist Max Weber (1864–1920) described the removal of myth and magic from social life as the "progressive disenchantment of the world," which was a result of secularization, rationalization, and the ascendancy of the scientific method (Green 2005). "Rationalization," in sociology, refers to a "long-term process whereby beliefs based on morality or superstition are replaced by rules and procedures based on logic and efficiency" (Bell 2013). Weber's German word for disenchantment, *Entzauberung*, is translated literally as "de-magicization." While Weber's primary focus was on the sociological function of disenchantment, he acknowledged it as a "philosophical act." A number of recent writers have focused primarily on the philosophical implications of disenchantment.

The backlash against disenchantment began with the Romanticists of the late 18th and early 19th centuries. This diverse group included artists, poets, composers, theologians, philosophers, and even some scientists. Most were pantheists, and they emphasized the individual, the transcendental, imagination, and a deep connection to nature. In recent years, there have been dozens of articles, essays, and books on "re-enchanting the world," and from almost as many perspectives. In the first three pages of an Amazon book search, I counted forty-four books with the word "re-enchantment" in the title. When I searched the word "re-enchanting," I found twenty-eight books listed in the first two pages. And yes, re-enchantment is mentioned specifically in conjunction with quantum physics, parapsychology, and panpsychism.

My journey through physics, philosophy, and parapsychology—and my search for the white crow—has brought me to a place of enchantment. Or perhaps re-enchantment. It has re-enchanted my later years with renewed feelings of wonder and connection to the Universe. In childhood, I started with an innate sense of the spiritual. Then I came to accept and internalize the scientific materialism of my family and the prevailing paradigm of the times. From my early teens through my early college years, I adopted a religious dualism. From college until my mid-thirties, I assumed a form of mysterianism (the notion that it is impossible to understand consciousness) and focused on the here and now of daily life. The death of my father in my mid-thirties reignited my search for ultimate answers, and my cancer diagnosis propelled me into my quest for white crows. I have now come to embrace a panpsychist view of reality and consciousness.

Similarly, early humans saw the world as imbued with spirit. Much of Eastern thought was essentially panpsychist, as was that of many of the early Greek philosophers. From there, prevailing Western thought moved towards a religious dualism that divorced consciousness from the material. Then, with Darwin in the mid-19th century, this dualism evolved (pun unintended) into the scientific materialism that prevails today—a view that has been predominant for less than 200 years. This materialistic monism that assumes consciousness is purely a product of brain function is beginning to give way to a philosophy of panpsychism. Quantum physics, in turn, makes room for this panpsychist view without it violating any laws of science. Evidence from parapsychology further supports panpsychism and even the possibility, and perhaps likelihood, of the survival of consciousness beyond death.

For me, the sheer logic-defying mystery of quantum physics (and its implications) evokes a sense of enchantment and awe. This, in combination with my examination of the various metaphysical models, places me unequivocally on the side of panpsychism. The only thing we know, or can know, with certainty is consciousness; and the reality of conscious experience itself is so mysterious that it is, in a sense, paranormal—beyond normal scientific understanding or explanation. I now believe that the intrinsic nature of the world, from the inside, is consciousness.

My study of the parapsychological literature and my several personal "white crow" experiences have convinced me of the reality of psychic phenomena. All of this does imply that the mind can perceive and act non-locally outside the brain. These conclusions are a necessary condition for the *possibility* of survival beyond death. However, they are not sufficient to prove there is an afterlife. And then there is the question of what that afterlife would look like; what exactly would survive?

If the nature of the universe is consciousness, then it is highly reasonable that some form of consciousness persists to at least unite with Universal Consciousness. This would not violate any laws of physics and could be entertained within a type of physicalist paradigm that incorporates physicalist panpsychism as described by Galen Strawson. Furthermore, if time does not exist in quantum reality, as some science suggests, then even after death, do I still exist in some-time or no-time? What does that even mean? How could that be the same me who experiences consciousness at this moment in space-time?

Could another me exist in another part of the "multiverse," as some have proposed? Again, what would that mean? That person may look like me and have my memories and personality, but would not experience my locus of consciousness. They would not be this consciousness that I experience in the moment. Maybe they are an actor channeling my personality, or someone with dissociative identity disorder who believes they are me. Maybe in my next life, I would have a different personality and different memories, but I would retain my sense of being "I." Perhaps I am not my memories or my personality, but my awareness in this moment of space-time, and this moment-by-moment awareness continues beyond brain death.

Merging with Universal Consciousness is very different from the personal survival implied by the "big five" phenomena described in the previous chapters. The anecdotal evidence and case reports supporting personal survival are compelling, especially when considered together. As we have seen, there is pushback against survival from both materialists and some skeptical parapsychologists. The materialists presuppose that the notions of both psi and an afterlife are absurd. The more agnostic parapsychologists wholeheartedly support the reality of psychic phenomena yet question personal survival. These survival skeptics, who believe in psi, base their skepticism on "super-psi" or living-agent psi.

On the face of it, especially when reading the extraordinary firsthand accounts of each of the five phenomena addressed, the survival hypothesis seems the most likely. Perhaps it is as simple as that. I don't believe it's truly possible to logically reason your way through the mysterious nature of matter and consciousness and arrive at certainty. For me, given the journey I've taken in life and in writing this book, it is more reasonable than not to believe in the continuation of consciousness, and indeed personal consciousness. I do feel, on a visceral level, that I am part of a greater cosmic conscious whole, and that has brought a sense of meaning.

So where do I go from here? I plan to refocus on the more mundane joys of daily living, which make this slice of space-time meaningful. I will get back to regular exercise and spend more time in nature, foraging for wild edibles on my nature walks. I'll devote more time to my family, both human and canine. With my written account now complete, I intend to continue my journey by exploring consciousness "from the inside" through personal, firsthand experience. I aim to develop a disciplined practice of meditation. If I overcome the trepidation, I may even try a guided psilocybin session, which has been shown in research to engender a mystical experience. (Many volunteers for such research "ranked their psilocybin experience as one of the most meaningful in their lives," even years later [Pollan 2019, p. 11].)

And now that I have worked through the science and philosophy and have chased my own white crow experiences, moving forward, I choose enchantment. Am I certain? No. There is little in this world that is certain. But perhaps certainty is not required. Perhaps it is enough to incline oneself towards the possible, or even the probable, especially when it brings a sense of meaning. So I will attempt to be less in my head. I will continue to explore, to seek, and to experience. And I will lean into Mystery.

Acknowledgments

I am indebted to many individuals who have influenced my thinking and supported me along my philosophical journey and in the writing of this book. First, I would like to thank the numerous authors who have contributed to my ideas, especially Dean Radin, whose books have had a profound effect on me.

I am grateful to Gené Fouché for taking the time to speak with me about method acting. Her insights regarding losing oneself in a role and her recommendation to watch the Jim Carrey movie *Man on the Moon* were invaluable.

Thank you to my friends Catie and Julie of Moon-Haven School of Magic in Frederick, MD. Their teaching on metaphysical subjects is unique and insightful. I truly value the experiences I've had in their classes.

I'd like to thank my good friend Peter Newman (who happens to be an English professor at Lafayette College) for providing his proofreading skills. He also told me a fun personal story about the time he participated in a parapsychology experiment as part of an audience of Grateful Dead concertgoers.

A special thanks to my brother Andy, with whom I had the good fortune to share my childhood. He helped write the book blurb/synopsis because I seem incapable of tooting my own horn.

And this book would not be what it is without the help and encouragement of my husband Bob. He listened with me, in the car, to countless hours of audiobooks on philosophy and physics and acted as consulting philosopher for the book.

Bibliography

Alex, Bridget. 2018. "The Human Brain Evolved to Believe in Gods." *Discover Magazine*. October 15, 2018. https://www.discovermagazine.com/planet-earth/the-human-brain-evolved-to-believe-in-gods.

Auerbach, Loyd. 2017. "Interactive Apparitions." In *Surviving Death* by Leslie Kean. Crown Publishing.

Ball, Philip. 2018. *Beyond Weird*. University of Chicago Press.

Barrett, Sir William. 1926. *Death-Bed Visions*. London: Methuen & Company.

Batthyány, Alexander. 2023. *Threshold*. St. Martin's Essentials.

Beischel, Julie. 2017. "Research into Mental Mediumship." In *Surviving Death* by Leslie Kean. Crown Publishing.

———. 2023. *The Reasonable Beyond: Valid Afterlife Evidence*. Kindle. The Windbridge Institute, LLC.

Bell, Kenton, ed. 2013. "Rationalization." In *Open Education Sociology Dictionary*. https://sociologydictionary. org/rationalization/.

Bering, Jesse. 2014 "One Last Goodbye: The Strange Case of Terminal Lucidity." *Scientific American Blog Network*. *Scientific American*. November 25, 2014. https://blogs.scientificamerican.com/bering-in-mind /one-last-goodbye-the-strange-case-of-terminal-luc idity/.

Braude, Stephen E. 2003. *Immortal Remains: The Evidence for Life After Death*. Maryland: Rowman & Littlefield Publishers.

———. 2021. "More Sloppy Reasoning about Survival." *Journal of Scientific Exploration*, 35 (3):477–84. https:/ /doi.org/10.31275/20212251.

Brook, Andrew, and Paul Raymont. 2021. "The Unity of Consciousness." *Stanford Encyclopedia of Philosophy Archive*: Summer 2021 Edition. https://plato.stanford .edu/archives/sum2021/entries/consciousness-unity/.

Brooks, Megan. 2022. "'Lucid Dying': EEG Backs Near-Death Experience During CPR." *Medscape*. November 7, 2022. https://www.medscape.com/viewar ticle/983675?form=fpf.

Broughton, Richard S. 1997. *Parapsychology, Philosophy, & Spirituality: A Postmodern Exploration (SUNY Series in Constructive Postmodern Thought)*. Albany, NY: State University of New York Press. From the back cover.

Buhlman, William. 1997. *Adventures Beyond the Body*. New York, NY: Harper Collins.

Capra, Fritjof. 1975. *The Tao of Physics*. Bantam Book.

Cook, Gareth. 2020. "Does Consciousness Pervade the Universe?" *Scientific American*. January 14, 2020. https://www.scientificamerican.com/article/does-consciousness-pervade-the-universe/.

Dalai Lama XIV. 2006. *The Universe in a Single Atom: The Convergence of Science and Spirituality*. Harmony.

De Quincey, Christian. 2003. "Data and the Divine." *IONS Noetic Sciences Review*, November.

Dewey, Russell A. 2018. "Multiple Personality," in Chapter 11 of *Psychology: An Introduction,* 2017–2018 Revision. *Psych Web* by Russ Dewey. Accessed January 21, 2024, from https://www.psywww.com/intropsych/ch11-personality/multiple-personality.html.

Docsa, V. P., & Szemán-Nagy, A. 2012. Szerepben lenni. Szinpadi szinészek disszociativ élményeinek vizsgálata "Be in role. Examination of dissociative experiences of theatrical actors." *Psychiatria Hungarica: A Magyar Pszichiatriai Tarsasag tudomanyos folyoirata*, 27(4), 255–262.

Eldadah, Basil A., Elena M. Fazio, and Kristina A. McLinden. 2019. "Lucidity in Dementia: A Perspective from the NIA." *Alzheimer's & Dementia*, no. 8 (August): 1104–6. https://doi.org/10.1016/j.jalz.2019.06.3915.

Elsaesser, Evelyn, Chris A. Roe, Callum E. Cooper, and David Lorimer. 2021. "The Phenomenology and Impact of Hallucinations Concerning the Deceased." *BJPsych Open*, no. 5 (August). https://doi.org/10.1192/bjo.2021.960.

Fenwick, Peter, Sue Brayne, and Hilary Lovelace. 2010. "Comfort for the Dying: Five Year Retrospective and One Year Prospective Studies of End-of-Life Experiences." *Archives of Gerontology and Geriatrics* vol. 51,2 (2010): 173–9. doi:10.1016/j.archger.2009.10.004.

Feynman, Richard P. 1965. *The Character of Physical Law.* MIT Press.

George, Alexander L., and Andrew Bennett. 2005. *Case Studies and Theory Development in the Social Sciences.* MIT Press.

Gimbel, Steven. 2020. *The Great Questions of Philosophy and Physics.* Chantilly, VA: The Teaching Company.

Goff, Philip. 2019. *Galileo's Error*. Vintage Books.

Goldstein, Rebecca Newberger. 2010. *36 Arguments for the Existence of God*. New York: Pantheon Books.

Gray, Dan. 2023. "Study Finds Evidence of Increased Brain Activity Right before Death." *Medical and Health Information. Medical News Today*. May 5, 2023.

Green, Jeffrey E. 2005. "Two Meanings of Disenchantment." *Philosophy and Theology*, no. 1: 51–84. https://doi.org/10.5840/philtheol2005171/24.

Greyson, Bruce. 2021. *After*. Bantam Press.

Gribbin, John. 1984. *In Search of Schrodinger's Cat*. New York, NY: Bantam Book.

Griffin, David Ray. 1997. *Parapsychology, Philosophy, & Spirituality: A Postmodern Exploration (SUNY Series in Constructive Postmodern Thought)*. Albany, NY: State University of New York Press.

———. 1998. *Unsnarling the World-Knot: Consciousness, Freedom, and the Mind-Body Problem*. Berkeley, Los Angeles and London: University of California Press.

Haraldsson, Erlendur, and Karlis Osis. 2012. *At the Hour of Death*. Revised. White Crow Books.

Henry, Richard Conn. 2005. "The Mental Universe." *Nature*, no. 7047 (July): 29–29. https://doi.org/10.1038/4 36029a.

Josephson, Brian. 1997. *The Conscious Universe*. First Edition. Harper Collins. From the back cover.

Kaiser, David. 2011. *How the Hippies Saved Physics: Science, Counterculture, and the Quantum Revival*. W. W. Norton & Company.

Kean, Leslie. 2017. *Surviving Death*. Crown Publishing.

Lund, David H. 1985. *Death and Consciousness*. McFarland & Company.

Maiese, Michelle. 2015. "Dissociative Identity Disorder and the Fragmentation of the Self," *Embodied Selves and Divided Minds, International Perspectives in Philosophy & Psychiatry* (Oxford, online edn, Oxford Academic, Dec. 1, 2015). Oxford University Press. https://doi.org/10.1092/med/9780199689231.003.0005.

Markovsky, Barry N., and Shane R. Thye. 2021. "Social Influence of Paranormal Beliefs." *University of South Carolina, Scholar Commons*. Spring 2021.

Mashour, G. A., Frank, L., Batthyany, A., Kolanowski, A. M., Nahm, M., Schulman-Green, D., Greyson, B., et al. 2019. Paradoxical lucidity: A potential paradigm shift for the neurobiology and treatment of severe dementias. *Alzheimer's & dementia : the journal of the Alzheimer's Association*, *15*(8), 1107–1114. https://doi.org/10.1016/j.jalz.2019.04.002.

Matlock, James G. 2022. "Criticisms of Reincarnation Case Studies." *Psi Encyclopedia*. London: The Society for Psychical Research. <https://psi-encyclopedia.spr.ac.uk/articles/criticisms-reincarnation-case-studies>.

———. 2022. "Clarifying Muddied Waters, Part 2: What the Sudduth-Tucker Debate About James Leininger Suggests For ReincarnatiResearch." *Journal of Scientific Exploration*, no. Winter 2022, Vol. 36, No. 4: 760–81. journalofscientificexploration.org.

Mendoza, Marilyn. 2018. "Why Some People Rally for One Last Goodbye Before Death." *Psychology Today*, October.

Monroe, Robert A. 1977. *Journeys Out of the Body*. New York, NY: DoubleDay.

Moody, Raymond A. 1976. *Life After Life*. New York, NY: Bantam Books.

Nagel, Thomas. 1974. "What Is It Like to Be a Bat?" *The Philosophical Review*.

Nahm, Michael. 2010. "Terminal Lucidity in People with Mental Illness and Other Mental Disability: An

Overview and Implications for Possible Explanatory Models." *Journal of Near-Death Studies*, December.

Parker, Clifton B. 2007. "Paranormal World Subject of Scrutiny." UC Davis. October 26, 2007. https://www.ucdavis.edu/news/paranormal-world-subject-scrutiny.

Parnia, Sam. 2006. *What Happens When We Die?: A Groundbreaking Study into the Nature of Life and Death*. Carlsbad, CA: Hay House, Inc.

Parnia, Sam, and Josh Young. 2013. *Erasing Death*. First Edition. New York, NY: Harper Collins.

Persinger, Michael. 1987. *Neuropsychological Bases of God Beliefs*. Praeger.

Pollan, Michael. 2019. *How to Change Your Mind*. Penguin.

Radin, Dean. 1997. *The Conscious Universe*. First Edition. New York, NY: Harper Collins.

———. 2004. "The Future Is Now." *Shift: At The Frontiers of Consciousness*, November.

———. 2006. *Entangled Minds*. New York, NY: Simon and Schuster.

———. 2018. *Real Magic*. First Edition. New York: Harmony Books.

Roach, Mary. 2006. *Spook: Science Tackles the Afterlife*. New York, NY: W. W. Norton & Company.

Rochat, Philippe. 2019. "Self-Unity as Ground Zero of Learning and Development." *Frontiers in Psychology*, March. https://doi.org/10.3389/fpsyg.2019.00414.

Rottenberg, Josh. 2017. "Jim Carrey on Losing Himself inside Andy Kaufman and Why He Relived It for the Documentary 'Jim & Andy.'" *- Los Angeles Times*. November 18, 2017. https://www.latimes.com/entertainment/movies/la-et-mn-jim-and-andy-20171118-htmlstory.html.

Ruickbie, Leo. 2023. *The Ghost in the Time Machine: The Survival of Human Consciousness After Permanent Bodily Death*. Kindle. Bigelow Institute for Consciousness Studies.

Sabom, Michael B. 1982. *Recollections of Death*. HarperCollins Publishers.

Sagan, Carl. 1996. *The Demon Haunted World*. Kindle. Ballantine Books.

Sartori, Penny. 2008. *The Near-Death Experiences of Hospitalized Intensive Care Patients*. Edwin Mellen Press.

Schwartz, Gary E., and William L. Simon. 2002. *The Afterlife Experiments*. New York, NY: Simon and Schuster.

Shermer, Michael. 2014. "Anomalous Events That Can Shake One's Skepticism to the Core." *Scientific American*, October.

Shroder, Tom. 1999. *Old Souls*. Simon and Schuster.

Soon, Chun Siong, Marcel Brass, Hans-Jochen Heinze, and John-Dylan Haynes. 2008. "Unconscious Determinants of Free Decisions in the Human Brain." *Nature Neuroscience*, no. 5 (April): 543–45. https://doi.org/10.1038/nn.2112.

Strasburger H, Waldvogel B. 2015. "Sight and blindness in the same person: Gating in the visual system." Psych J. 2015 Dec;4(4):178-85. doi: 10.1002/pchj.109. Epub 2015 Oct 15. PMID: 26468893.

Strawson, Galen. 2018. "The Consciousness Deniers." *NYR Daily/The New York Review of Books*, April.

Sudduth, Michael. 2015. "Personal Reflections on Life after Death." *Cup of Nirvana*. https://www.facebook.com/profile.php?id=100004468214909. August 7, 2015. https://michaelsudduth.com/personal-reflections-on-life-after-death/.

———. 2021. "The James Leininger Case Re-Examined." *Journal of Scientific Exploration*. https://doi.org/https://doi.org/10.31275/20212359.

Sullivan, Will. 2023. "Surging Brain Activity in Dying People May Be a Sign of Near-Death Experiences." Smart News. *Smithsonian Magazine.* May 5, 2023.

Treffert, D. A., & Treffert, D. A. 2021. "The Sudden Savant: A New Form of Extraordinary Abilities." *WMJ: official publication of the State Medical Society of Wisconsin, 120*(1), 69–73.

Tucker, Jim B. 2016. "The Case of James Leininger: An American Case of the Reincarnation Type." *Explore* (NY). 2016 May–Jun; 12(3):200–7. doi: 10.1016/j.explore.2016.02.003. Epub 2016 Mar 2. PMID: 27079216.

———. 2017. "Investigating Cases of Children with Past-Life Memories." In *Suriving Death* by Leslie Kean. Crown Publishing.

———. 2022. "Response to Sudduth's 'James Leininger Case Re-Examined.'" *Journal of Scientific Exploration.*

Utts, Jessica. 1991. "Replication and Meta-Analysis in Parapsychology." *Statistical Science*, no. 4 (November). https://doi.org/10.1214/ss/1177011577.

———. 2016. "Appreciating Statistics." *Journal of the American Statistical Association* 111 (516): 1373–80. doi:10.1080/01621459.2016.1250592.

———. 2019. "An Assessment of the Evidence for Psychic Functioning." *Journal of Parapsychology*, 82, no. 3

(May): 118–46. https://doi.org/10.30891/jopar.2018s. 01.10.

Vlahos, Hadley. 2023. *The In-Between*. Ballantine Books.

Wehrstein, KM. 2017. "James Leininger (reincarnation case)." *Psi Encyclopedia*. London: The Society for Psychical Research.<https://psi-encyclopedia.spr.ac.uk/ articles/james-leininger-reincarnation-case>.

———. (2018). "Philip Psychokinesis Experiments." *Psi Encyclopedia*. London: The Society for Psychical Research. <https://psi-encyclopedia.spr.ac.uk/articles/ philip-psychokinesis-experiments>.

"What Is Humanism? » Understanding Humanism." n.d. Understanding Humanism. Accessed April 10, 2022, from https://understandinghumanism.org.uk/ what-is-humanism/.

Windt, Jennifer M., Tore Nielsen, and Evan Thompson. 2016. "Does Consciousness Disappear in Dreamless Sleep?" *Trends in Cognitive Sciences*, no. 12 (December): 871–82. https://doi.org/10.1016/j.tics.2016.09.006.

Wolfe, Tom. 1968. *The Electric Kool-Aid Acid Test*. New York: Picador.